I CAME IN HERE FOR A REASON

I Came in Here for a Reason

More Ramblings in
Retirement

SHELLEY ANN DOUTHETT

Other titles by author:

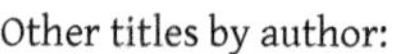

Did I Say That Out Loud? Ramblings in Retirement (2018)

All photos were taken by the author unless otherwise noted and then used by permission of the photographer, as noted.

Cover Artwork-amazingly real bird drawings by the author; design by talented and patient Eileen Clarke and the author.

ISBN/SKU 979-8-218-19598-4
EISBN 979-8-218-19600-4

CONTENTS

This book is dedicated to Joseph Kitty. My muse and partner in writing. He sat alongside me through every story in my first book and most of the this one. Any time I got stuck, I'd just scratch his head, (instead of mine) and move on. He was a creative genius. One day in April 2020, he didn't show up and after a lot of searching and sadness, I realized he was gone for good. Thanks Joseph, for being part of my life for 10 years. I miss you every day.

ACKNOWLEDGEMENTS

There are so many people who have helped me become a better writer over the years. They've also put up with the many drafts of each story. They encourage and provide meaningful feedback to which I mostly listen. Grudgingly. It serves them right that I can't stop writing. I've been part of a group called the First Wednesday Writing Class for over a decade and the members of our core group are now family. Instructors Eileen Clarke and John Barsness have taught me more about writing than I realized I could learn. Both have hair that has gone gray since I joined the class. Classmates John LaRue, Bev Monigal, Matt Nelson, and Diane Johnson Freuh. They were already gray because they are older than me. Each provide honest feedback knowing I desperately need it. Thank you all for keeping me on track and trying to manage my issues with focus. Most of all, thank you for your friendship.

My editing staff is comprised of friends who are not afraid to tell the truth and do not use red pens to point out problems. My friend who really should be an editor, Mark Lanier, sees everything at the point where I think I'm done and points out quite clearly and kindly where I need to clarify, rework something, and even change the titles of different stories. He's my go to guy. Thanks Nerd.

After I get through Mark's edits, I cajole or shamelessly beg people I know to go through it all and catch all my mistakes and read for content so that you, the reader, will love it. They are Angie

Janacaro, Dawn Reynolds, Kay Ingalls, Lee Weldon, Jeanne West, Roxann LaRue, and Eileen Clarke. Thank you everyone!!

When I needed help with the pictures and cover, I turned to my son in law, Tom Ajello, a true master of creative design. I asked him for some kind of program that would allow me to use filters to enhance the artistry and keep the pictures clearer than my first book had. He suggested Be Funky. I downloaded it and then spent an inordinate amount of time playing around with pictures. It was so fun. I did the artwork for the cover with a pencil and piece of paper, took a picture of it and transformed it into something I really love. Then Eileen and I made a cover. Thank you Tom and Eileen!

I probably wouldn't have written a second book had I not gotten such great feedback from the first book. All of you who read that one gave me the confidence and courage to press on. I thank all of you, the readers, for allowing me to share my life and strange tales with you. Having you in my back pocket makes it all worth it.

THE INTERLOPERS

Does it look like I like them?

The best day of my life happened the moment I was born. I don't remember anything about it but I just know it was. Yeah, I had the cord wrapped around my neck and I was blue but other than that, it was a banner day for me.

I am the firstborn of four. For almost thirteen months, I was the center of my parent's lives. I know this because there are a LOT of pictures of me looking extremely adorable. From what I can tell, I smiled a lot in those days. I had a magnificent hairdo everyday involving gathering up most of my hair and putting it in a little ponytail that stuck out of the top of my head. I call it the 'palm tree.'

I got to spend all my time with Mom or Dad or both. Dad and I drove around in their convertible, me standing next to him, holding onto his shoulder. He was so proud. I was so happy. Yeah, I know. There weren't baby seats or even seat belts back then. Dad taught me to play football and there is a great picture of me trying to hike a full-sized football while wearing just a cloth diaper, looking back at the camera, while waiting for him to tell me to hike the ball. I probably fell on my face if I was able to actually attempt it. Mom and I spent a lot of time bonding too. She let me play in the cupboards and didn't get mad when I took every pot and pan out, happily banging away. We went for walks and I wore stylish dresses. She was beautiful and I was cute, the perfect pair. I was even featured in a two-page spread in the Armed Forces newspaper, Stars and Stripes. Fame for a couple minutes.

Ah yes, those were the days.

Then one day, Mom disappeared for a while and showed back up with this thing that needed pretty much all of her attention. It was my new baby brother, Bruce, and at first, I was confused. I learned to accept him. The hundreds of pictures taken of us together support this. He was not an attractive baby so I was still the cutest. I have evidence.

It took me about a year to come to terms with this addition to our little family. I actually liked him more than I thought I would, most of the time. Then we moved from Kadena Air Force base in Okinawa to Otis Air Force base near Cape Cod, Massachusetts and Mom disappeared for a few more days. Uh oh.

Once again, she came home with another thing, sister Tracey, that took all her attention. Attention I was pretty sure I still deserved. Unfortunately for me, and unlike my brother, this thing was cute. It was getting to be too much. Since I was only 2, I had no control over my life and therein lies the rub.

For almost two years, I spent a lot of time working on important things like acceptance of these wiggly, poopy, hungry little people that kept popping up in my world. And getting potty trained. Neither one was very easy.

When I turned 4, I thought I had made great strides in the big sister department. I had helped with feeding Bruce and Tracey, shared my toys sometimes, and worked hard on developing the fine art of blaming them for anything I did where I might get into trouble.

And then one day, Mom disappeared again. Why does this keep happening?

When Dad got off work, he piled the 3 of us into our station wagon and off we went to the hospital to see Mom. When we got there, she showed us our new baby sister, Wendy, who was lying blissfully in a bassinet, looking sweet and adorable. Drat. Another cute one.

So, what did I do? I leaned over the bassinet and sneezed. After a few days finally being at home, littlest sister went back into the hospital with pneumonia. I promise I wasn't trying to kill her. What does a 4- year-old know about germs? She survived and I was very relieved.

Any family having more than one child has trouble with which one has it the easiest or hardest. Birth order is a complicated and studied phenomenon. There are lots of books written about it and they are all wrong. It's way more personal than putting us in boxes based on what order we were born. I know, for a fact, that being born first is the hardest.

When I was in junior high school I was in the choir. We were about to have our first big concert and we were all given these matching blue vests to wear with instructions to wear a black skirt, white shirt and dress shoes. It would be my first experience wearing nylons. After I put them on, all the hairs on my legs were either smashed down or sticking through them. It was very uncomfortable. So, I asked Mom if I could finally shave my legs. She said no because she thought I was too young to start.

Because I was kind of bad about taking no for an answer, especially for something this critical in my adolescent life, I snuck into Dad's shaving kit and got his razor. It was one of those 'safety' razors where the blade sticks out of two sides. I shut and locked the door to the bathroom, climbed into the tub and got my legs wet and soapy. I proceeded to run the razor up my shin. This is where instruction from a practiced adult would have been handy. A long strip of skin came up with the razor. Blood poured into the tub. I stifled a scream. I hadn't been aware that my fear of getting caught would manifest itself in the amount of pressure I put on the razor and instead of shaving the hairs off my leg, I dug a trough. For whatever reason, the takeaway still resonating in my brain, even today, is why it is called a 'safety' razor.

Why is this sad tale so important to birth order? Both of my sisters got to shave at much younger ages than I did. At some point, Mom figured she had bigger parenting battles to deal with and in this case she'd have someone able to show them how **not** to do it. This proved to be a common theme throughout our growing up years.

As the oldest, I was held to a higher standard called *'You Are An Example'* and from then on, I had to provide guidance regarding what to do or not to do in the world of Right and Wrong behavior. I hadn't asked for this when I was born and rebelled mightily. Who, in their right mind, would want to be so responsible all the time? Not I. So, I began a campaign to do things Wrong. I think I did them Wrong just to get attention but my actions also served a greater purpose to my younger siblings of what happens if you get caught doing a Wrong thing. It was painful in many ways but at least I got noticed.

Even when I didn't do something wrong, I got blamed for stuff. On my 13th birthday, my sisters were tossing a tennis ball in the house, a major no-no. One of them missed catching the ball and it bounced and landed on this little brass boat on the coffee table and broke off the little umbrellas. When questioned about what happened, it ended up being my fault because I should have known better. Wait, what? I'm not sure I was even in the room when it happened. And it was my birthday.

Oh, I could go on and on about the injustices of life as the oldest but what's the point? I actually love the interlopers more than I ever expected to. No matter their transgressions, whether I was blamed or not, or their annoying habits coming from all of us living together for so many years, I actually missed them a lot when I went off to college which surprised me. And I have especially missed them after we all took off to live our individual lives because we literally scattered to the winds. I've even forgiven my parents who were so mean to me by giving me so much responsibility. How could they know what it's like to be the oldest when they were both the babies of their families?

When we all get together from time to time, we spend a lot of time remembering our growing up days and it is interesting how different each of our perspectives are about some event long ago. It's like putting together a puzzle when all four of us work out the details of some memory of a place we lived. And putting all those little bits of our history together is part of what I look forward to most during our infrequent gatherings.

While working on my stories, I sometimes send out a message to the interlopers to keep me honest. It was sister Wendy who owned up to hitting the brass boat with a tennis ball and what she remembered was how Mom got mad at me since I was the oldest and should have known better. I still don't see the logic in it. And when I was trying to remember the details of whatever board or card games we played as a family, everyone fondly remembered our Tripoley nights and the tablecloth Dad had painted for it.

Even though I didn't ask for them to be born, I have also forgiven them. That's the kind of sister I am. They've managed to grow on me and I wouldn't trade them for anything in the world. In fact, I freely admit I love them more than I ever thought possible. I am only somewhat damaged by being so responsible but I'll take it.

I can guarantee one or all of the interlopers
will find something they don't like about
themselves in this photo. Any bets?

MINING THE PAST

Not sure if this is the guy who fathered 16 kids but he is quite handsome.
I think I got his bedhead hair style. And eyebrows.

I've managed to come up with a new addiction and I blame my Little Mother. Again.

A couple Christmas's ago, I came up with the brilliant idea to get Little Mother a year's subscription to Ancestry.com. She is at the age where she has enough material stuff and I didn't want to add to it plus she always says she doesn't need anything. I'm learning to be creative in the gift giving department.

Mom had been going through some of her things and had found a manila envelope with a bunch of papers copied from someone about her mother's family history. There were things about her grandparents and great grandparents and a farm in Wisconsin. Sister Tracey (who is not a nun) had already done some family history on her own, as had our maternal grandmother. It was a mish-mash of history and it seemed like a good idea to set up a family tree in Ancestry. Also, this way, all of us could look at it and work on it.

I wasn't sure Mom would just jump on her computer and start working on her family history. She does pretty well with her email and newsfeed stuff but there is a bit of a learning curve for building a family tree so I decided to try it first so I could explain to her how it works and what to do.

I got onto the site, did a few tutorials and got busy. It didn't take long before I was hooked. In no time at all, I had over 300 people added and it started to take shape. The fun thing about the Ancestry program is how it pulls hints from its databases for people as you add relatives. They appear as little green leaves next to a person in the tree. They could be census records, city directories, church records, military records, and a whole bunch of other things. The more I worked on it, the more hints popped up and before long, hours had passed and I had a crazed look on my face. Now I understand what cats feel like with catnip. I was excited for Christmas!!

My brilliant idea turned out to have a few flaws. While my laptop computer was relatively new, Mom's old Mac computer didn't have the ability to pull up the screen showing the tree. What? It showed everything else the Ancestry site had but not the tree. Some dumb file error kept showing up making me say bad words under my breath. After a little research, I discovered the problem was that the old Mac couldn't be updated anymore and the only way to fix it was to get a new one. Uh oh.

Little Mother did not want a new one. She loved her old one, even though it didn't quite work sometimes. I adopted a new strategy while I made not so subtle hints about how a new computer would be so much better. I continued to add to the tree from my computer and would call her up and tell her all the things I found. Sometimes she would throw in remarks about what she remembered about a few of the people I had added and I'd write them down and later add them to the notes in the Ancestry program.

Once, when I built a part of the tree that showed her great grandfather on her mother's side, we had the following conversation:

Me: *Mom, I found out your great grandfather had 16 kids.*
Mom: *How is that possible?*
Me: *Um, he was a horndog.*
Mom: *Shelley Ann, who taught you to talk like that?*
Me: *I'm sorry but, this guy had one wife who gave him 9 children and then she died so he married another woman who also gave him 7 more kids.*
Mom: *I see what you mean.*
Me: *And you know what else?*
Mom: *I'm not sure I want to know.*

Me: *His second wife was pregnant with their first child before his first wife died.*

Silence.

It's been the gift that keeps on giving. We now have over two thousand people in our tree. Hints keep pouring in and we keep chasing them. It's hard to stay focused because my eyes dry out and I've had to go back and delete people because I either got something wrong or I was adding people who had no blood ties to us. It's hard to delete people. I feel like I'm killing them even though I didn't since most of them have already died.

It all seemed so straight forward when I started. I put in our family. Then I added Mom and Dad's parents, and then I found their parents who had a bunch of kids. So, then I tracked those kids to their families. Lo and behold, I have a whole new group of cousins and aunts and uncles. Words describing their relationship to me are confusing. What the heck is a 2nd cousin twice removed? Removed from what? If I think about it too much, it makes my eyes cross. Seriously.

After the Christmas present with all these new family connections, Mom decided to do the Ancestry DNA test. She has always been proud of her Norwegian heritage and was convinced she was 100% Norwegian. In looking at the tree, I can see why she thought so because we found a lot of people back a few generations in the Old Country. Imagine her surprise to find she has other countries in her DNA like Sweden, Denmark and Greenland. I made some not very helpful remark about how the Vikings were known for sailing around, raping and pillaging villages, and just causing all kinds of mayhem. It's just how the world worked back then. No one is a 100% if you go back far enough.

Speaking of going back far enough, I literally hit the wall when I got to the generations that came from other countries. Surnames were almost impossible to make sense of in Norway because everyone is a dotter (for girls) or a sen (for boys) so the root of the surname is after the father. What about the mother?! She did all the work.

So, our great, great, great grandfather was Sjur Larrsen Dorheim which means he was Lars's son. And his wife was Ragnelea Olsdotter which means her dad's last name was Olsen. Where did Dorheim come from? Turns out it's the name of the town his dad was from. Then, Sjur had a son so his last name was Sjurson. I keep getting headaches when I work on the Norwegian part of the family.

When they all emigrated to the United States, they Americanized their names, making it somewhat harder to find where they all went. Family lore has it that when Lars Sjurson emigrated, he heard someone say their surname was Gaard and he liked that better so he changed his name to Gaard and that is why my mom's maiden name is Gaard. I have no idea if this is true.

Since my eyes threatened to stay permanently crossed, I got out of Mom's side of the tree and headed over to Dad's. It didn't take many generations before I was frustrated by the fact that the same names were used in every generation. David, Alexander, Benjamin, and Joseph. Sometimes, if a Benjamin died before the age of one, they named another son Benjamin. This happened with several of the aforementioned names. Come on.

Dad's 5th great grandfather, Joseph, took a ship from Ireland in 1790 and he eventually made it to Pennsylvania where he stayed. The subsequent Davids, Josephs, Alexanders and Benjamins married and had lots of kids. Guess what many of their names were. For the most part, they were farmers and blacksmiths and the Presbyterian church was their religion of choice. We have parts of a book about Butler County, north of Pittsburgh that talks about the role of our family in the area so we know there was a family farm with a family cemetery. We have a few pictures of the patriarchy who were heavily involved in the church and they look really stern and a bit scary.

Recently, Sister Tracey (who is not a nun), daughter Megan, and I went to Northern Ireland to chase down Dad's relatives. We knew they came from County Armagh but we didn't know where in the county or how far back we could go. Turned out, we couldn't find anybody. The genealogy center was closed while we were in Belfast. So, we headed to Armagh and went to several cemeteries. Not a Douthett (*pronounced Dow thit) to be found. Logic told us Joseph wasn't the only Douthett in Ireland so where were the rest? We didn't have enough time to find out.

From a genealogy standpoint, the trip wasn't really a bust. Granted, we didn't find what we were looking for but we soaked up a lot of history and a sense of the country. Already we want to go back.

I think what has surprised me the most in this whole ancestor search thing, is all the emotions I've felt while digging through the records. There's sadness in the loss families must have felt when a child died as a child and not as an adult. Way too many of these. Or what a mother went through when her husband died and left her with children too young to work. What did she do to support them? I feel like I want to hug them.

I am humbled by these people, in what they managed to accomplish. They farmed, they owned land, they had businesses, they fought in wars. They worked hard for everything they had. Hard in those days is nothing like hard today and I have a deep appreciation for what it must have been like. I'm not sure I could handle the physical stamina needed to live every day.

In the meantime, I'll keep digging and imagining the lives of these people. Who knows, I might find a real Viking in our history. I wonder who kept records for them. But the real surprise here is how did I know I would also be a recipient of this gift? I'm sure Little Mother appreciated it but I feel like I know myself a little bit better.

I'm brilliant! Must be genetics.

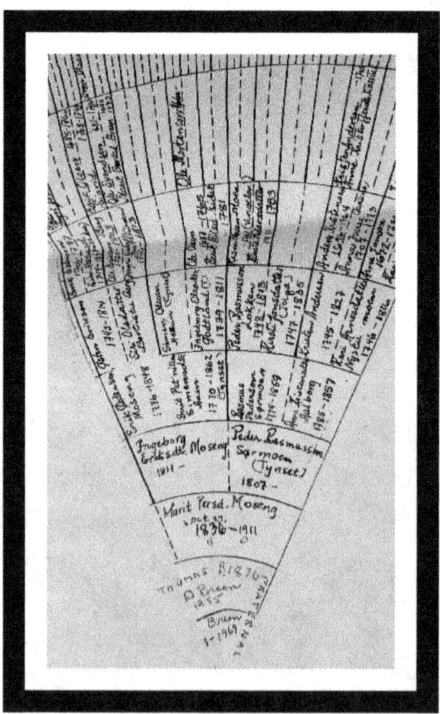

No wonder we wanted to put this in Ancestry.

~ 3 ~

TALLY HO!

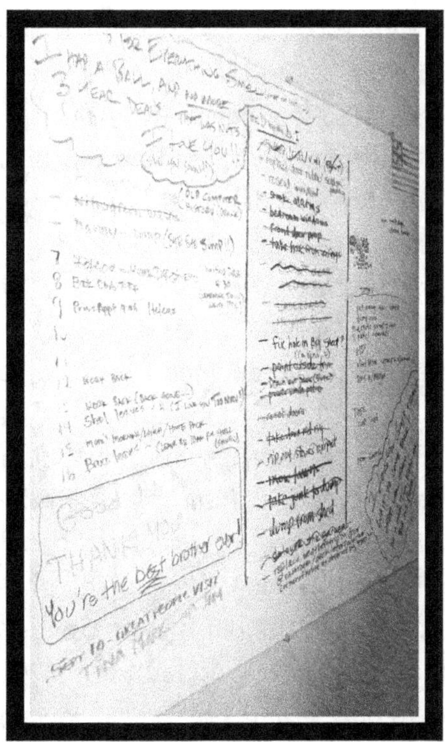

The giant white board is not only useful for tallying.
Everyone who comes to visit adds their own touch to it.
It's become a community white board where the only rule is to
be nice.

I'm trying to decide if I have yet another problem. The problem with finding out if I have a problem is figuring out what to do about it, just in case I determine I do have a problem. Let me set the stage so you can see what I mean.

Real life scenario #1- I have just finished making my bed. I notice there is something on my dresser that doesn't belong there. I pick it up and head to another part of the house to put it away. Along the way, I remember I need to get to the post office to mail something I meant to send last week. I stop. I am standing in the middle of the kitchen wondering why I came in here. I try to remember where I was heading in the first place. I look at the thing in my hand and wonder why it's there and why I stopped in the middle of the kitchen. The thing I'm holding is providing me with no clues.

Real life scenario #2- I've decided I need to dust. Now that's a miracle in itself and I feel like I've made an important choice about the thing I really want to accomplish today. (Dusting is a chore only slightly more appealing to me than cleaning toilets.) I walk from the living room to the pantry where I keep all the cleaning supplies. When I get there, I stop. I have arrived at the place I was meaning to go. So far, so good. I scan the pantry, waiting for inspiration. Am I here to get something to eat or do laundry or WHY AM I HERE? I have no idea but I'm sure whatever it was, was a good idea at the time, literally seconds ago. *(insert primal scream of frustration)* Maybe it's just not a good dusting day and some inner voice is telling me to find something more fun to do. Again.

Real life scenario #3- I'm working on a project in a bedroom I've been remodeling. All I have left to do is the trim and baseboards. I just need a drill, a hammer, some small nails, a tape measure, and the wood for the trim. I move from the workroom to the bedroom, carrying what I thought were all of those things. Nope. I forgot the drill bits. Drat. I go back into the workroom and stop. Why am I here? There's something I was supposed to get. I trudge back to the bedroom, frantically searching my brain for the one thing I needed. When I get to the bedroom, I notice the drill. THE BITS!! Whew. I race back to the workroom, pick up the bits and with a smile on my face, return to the bedroom. Why do I feel like I have just won the Publisher's Clearinghouse Sweepstakes?

Real life scenario #4- I walk into the grocery store to get one or two specific things like milk and a bag of ready to eat salad. As soon as I get in the door, my mind goes blank. Why am I here? What do I need? Those one or two things were so critical, I had to leave my house and race into town to get them and now I am standing in the store, still as a statue. I'm hoping no one asks me if I need help because I might actually tell them how much and what kind I really need. They may feel the need to bring in men in white coats and soothing voices. Oh dear.

It happens that quickly. That thing I do several times a day, where I have some minor task and in the course of doing it, I blank out. I know I came in here for a reason but I have no idea what it was. Sound familiar?

As this behavior becomes more commonplace, I wonder if it's getting worse or I'm just more aware of it for some reason. I wonder if I'm losing parts of my brain. I wonder if there's anything I can do about it. I decide to tally up the number of times it occurs in any one day for at least a week to see if I need to be concerned. I find a blank spot on my whiteboard and write in the days of the week. I will mark down every time I walk into a room and forget what I was there for.

While I'm here at the whiteboard, I decide to update my to-do list. I carry a myriad of things to do in my brain throughout the day and at the end of said day, none of them get done. Sometimes it feels like nothing ever gets done. I pick out the marker I had just put back, move the two steps from marker bucket to whiteboard, and stand there. What are those things I meant to add to my to-do list? Where did they go in the great abyss of my brain? As I sigh in frustration yet again and begin to walk away, one of those things pops into my head and I quickly turn around and write it down. Whew. Crisis averted. While I'm patting myself on the back, another thing pops up and then another. Pretty soon I have a daunting list and wish I hadn't thought it was such a good idea.

This counts as my first tally mark for the day. It then hits me that I don't know what day of the week it is. This is a common phenomenon in retirement. I start laughing. I quickly make a mark on Tuesday, hoping it really **is** Tuesday, and shake my head. Already I can see there may be some flaws in potential data gathering. Since I'm the only one who really cares about the data, I resolve to just do the best I can.

Well, this idea didn't even last the week. There weren't as many tally marks as I thought there would be and I swear it wasn't because I forgot to make them. I realized I needed to cut myself some slack. If I was really worried about my state of mind, I'd sit down and focus on being focused. Do some breathing exercises. Maybe what I really needed do was to pay attention to how many times I walked into a room and actually knew what I was doing there. And when that happened, I should do some kind of victory dance.

Tally Ho just became Tally No.

~ 4 ~

MY FRIEND EVOLUTION

I didn't start out in life successfully keeping friends for long. I blame my Dad. As an Air Force brat, I moved a lot for the first 15 years of my life and spilled a lot of tears saying goodbye to friends I met in all the different schools and bases. Sadly, I probably met hundreds of kids but only remember a few names.

I've thought a lot about the whole friend journey in terms of my evolution in becoming a fairly decent human being. Starting over in a new place never stopped me from finding more willing victims, I mean friends. I really honed my skills in second grade when we moved twice and I ended up in three different classrooms. There is nothing like walking into a new classroom and getting introduced to everyone while standing at the front, knees shaking, and feeling all those eyes on me. By middle school, I was a seasoned pro. It was never easy, it just got easier. Then Dad retired and we moved one last time.

This move was in my sophomore year of high school to a rural small town in northern California where everyone had grown up and known each other since birth. It was not only awkward to be the new kid again, but to be the new kid in a non-military background school was mortifying. After some bumbling and fumbling in the first year there, I decided it was a lot easier to be friends with everyone than be part of a group like jocks, brains, popular, stoners, or loners. I think I was a floater, if I had to name it.

Whatever I was, I survived and decades later I still have friends from that time period. I love them for hanging in there with me for so long. I enjoy their company when we actually see each other every so often. Our journeys in life since that long-ago time may not give us much in common, but with age comes genuine friendship. The things that bind us now are in the transitions of life we all have in common: aging parents, health issues, retirement, family drama, etc. I've received heartfelt words of support and encouragement from people I haven't seen more than a couple of times in decades. How cool is that?

In college, I picked up a few more lifetime friends and I get to see them a lot more often. What holds us together was forged in the survival that was the whole college experience. We have a real history now and I don't see them ever not being an important part of my life. I constantly remind them they are stuck with me. So far, no one has run screaming from the room.

After college, I got a job with the US Forest Service. This opened up another revolving door of both work and community friends. I got to work in Utah, Idaho, and Montana, mostly in rural communities. Again, it wasn't easy fitting into communities of multi-generational roles and history. And because I worked for the federal government, there were places where I was a hard sell. Everyone, including me, has had a rocky relationship with the government rules and regulations. Using my seasoned pro skills, I looked for a common thread. It was either that or spend my time twiddling my thumbs or learning something useful like canning vegetables or crocheting. I did both but it didn't fill the need to connect with people. I have a low tolerance for loneliness. Been there, done that.

So, in one community it was playing in a women's basketball league, and in another, it was group hiking, camping and exploring. My rancher friends made me a lot better horseback rider and I learned to 'help' with branding, feeding and vaccinating livestock. I'm pretty sure I will never need another vaccination for any cattle related illness for the rest of my life, as I managed to vaccinate myself more than a few times. I'm fine. Mostly.

Somewhere along the timeline of my life, I went from being a bit of an introvert to crazy woman, in your face, questionable filter extrovert. Now, in my 60s, I'm pretty comfortable chatting with just about anyone who gets within range. I am fascinated by the stories of the people I come in contact with almost daily. I don't have to know their whole history, just enough to feel like I'll know how to approach them should we cross paths again. As an added plus, people are just plain interesting. The biggest surprise during this phase of my life is how easy it is to just strike up a conversation. There are always subtle commonalities, some life experience we have shared, or a common interest in some aspect of life.

I was once camped in an RV park in Beatty, Nevada just outside of Death Valley National Park. Two encounters from the trip have stayed with me for years. I had stopped in Furnace Creek to take a look at the golf course and happened to run into a woman working there wearing a shirt from Yellowstone. I started a conversation with her about it and the next thing I knew, we had scheduled a tee time and a place my dogs could hang out while we golfed. I wasn't prepared for what it's like to golf 81 feet below sea level. It suffices to say, if you like hitting rocks with a golf club, this is the place for you. That's what it felt like every time I hit the ball. The course was absolutely beautiful. Like golfing at an oasis. A chance conversation turned into an unexpected and amazing experience.

My other fun encounter there had to do with some people parked near me in the RV park. Every day I would come back from exploring different parts of Death Valley and find the same group sitting in chairs outside their campers, drinking beer and laughing. And every day I said hello. They were very friendly and nice about my doggies who wanted to visit them periodically. One day, I was getting something out of my truck when one of the guys got up and headed towards the shower building. I have no idea what I was thinking when I said, *'I can't believe your wife lets you go out in public with legs that white.'* Everyone started laughing. I'm sure he had a witty comeback but I didn't hear it. After that, we were buddies.

Unlike the first 15 years of my life when I left friends and never saw them again, I now have friends who pop in and out of my world and make it better. We pick up right where we left off.

A few years ago I stopped at an old friend's house on my way to visit family a few states away. I hadn't seen her in many years. We got caught up on each other's lives and off I went. About a year later she called and asked if I wanted to go on a raft trip down the Main Salmon River. Uh, yeah! So off I went with a whole bunch of people I didn't know and one I did. By the end of the trip, I had a bunch of new friends, two of which were young men who had gone to college together, went on with their separate lives and decided to do this river trip together. Jens and Kevin hadn't seen each other much since then but the trip cemented their friendship even more as they threw barbs back and forth, somehow managing to include the rest of us. Before long, it felt like we had known them all our lives. By the time we all went back to our real lives, I wanted to adopt them except they already had moms. Rats.

I did feel like I could give them motherly advice so that made me feel better. I may never see them again but if I do, we will relive our fun times on the river, where they pulled me into a raft after I'd gotten bucked out of my kayak in a particularly evil rapid. They didn't even make comments about how I looked like a drowned rat or weighed about a million pounds. That's what friends do. Or guys who respect their mothers.

Whitewater rafting has brought me many new friends but sometimes it's the old friends who make it happen. Nanette, one of my high school friends I hadn't seen since those long ago days invited Sister Tracey *(who is not a nun)*, and me on a trip on the San Juan River. Her group had run rivers together for years and since Tracey and I were a formidable double kayak team, we said yes. The next several days we blasted through Class 3 and 4 rapids in a flotilla of rafts and kayaks, set up and took down camp as we made our way down the river, fixed yummy meals and hiked some of the most beautiful country in the world. Moments and scenes from the trip are forever etched in my brain and the new friends are now part of my heart.

The friends I have in my little town add so much to my everyday life, it's hard to define in words. Actions speak louder than words and the friends I have here are deafening. It's why I've had to get hearing aids. I even have a friend who yells at me if I don't wear them.

For about 2 years, I had a problem with my hot water heater. Since it took a long time to get all the kinks worked out, I availed myself of showers at many of my friend's houses. I tried not to keep going to the same place all the time so I changed it up and discovered a whole myriad of different kinds of showerheads, soaps, and empathy. I never once, had to ask a perfect stranger if I could shower at their house. It was offered up freely by my newly designated *best* friends. I was going to say shower best friends but that conjures up more than me borrowing their showers and well, no.

My golfing friends take friendship to a whole new level. Our first year or so we played here at home and it was more of a get out and move kind of activity. We all play either really good or really bad, usually a hole at a time. One good shot begets at least one bad shot and so it goes all the way to the end. We've all run out of positive reinforcement phrases so sometimes we have to tell it like it is. We laugh. A lot. Hitting trees on the course happens frequently. One time I was standing a long way behind the group because I didn't want to die. We had already seen Iris hit two people that year and it felt like a good strategy to stand back. (*So as not to cause undue embarrassment, I changed her name*) I saw her ball hit a tree. It actually climbed the tree, ran up and across a large branch and fell behind her. I laughed so hard I had to find the course bathroom soon thereafter. It was touch and go for a moment.

We've traveled the state playing new to us golf courses. Laughter and cusswords can be heard up and down the fairways everywhere we go. A nice meal and an adult beverage can be had everywhere we go, and we relive every hysterical moment. Sometimes photos help with the telling. These friends are the gifts that just keep giving.

I've been in my little town for over 30 years and I've got so many friends, I sometimes blank out on some names. I keep adding friends like some kind of addiction. Rotary, book club, adult ed classes, school activities, shopping at the local stores and the list goes on. I've become this person who others might describe as '*she never met a stranger.*'

I've come a long way since I was born so many years ago. From the Air Force years of fleeting friendships, to developing and keeping friends, or even letting some go with peace of mind. My now personal favorite has become engaging with some random person who looks like they need a kind word. It's what I have become, Ms. Chatty.

I can hardly wait to see where I go from here.

~ 5 ~

I KNOW THAT SMELL!

Of all the senses, I've come to realize that the sense of smell can be the most powerful of all. It can bring me to my knees or light up my world. My reactions to a smell range anywhere from dry heaves to tears. This story isn't about the bad smells though. It's about life smells. The ones bringing up a memory of a place or a person or a time period in life.

When my grandmother died many years ago, Dad, Mom, my sisters and I made a final trip to the house Dad mostly grew up in. It was located in San Gabriel, California and was built when the area was nothing but orange groves. Both the front and back yards had several trees left from the orchards, and the smell of them, especially in the morning dew, was magical. Orange tree bark smell was different than orange tree leaves smell which was different than the actual oranges smell. They all came together to mean we were at our grandparent's. Summer childhood memories came flooding back.

As we wandered through the house on that final trip, my sisters and I went through a litany of 'remember when' moments of our childhood. Our family had made a trip there every year from the time I can remember to my college days. We drove from wherever we were stationed in the Air Force, to the little house in San Gabriel, to descend on our grandparents for a week or more of creating chaos in their lives. Those poor people. What great times.

After all that time, Grandma's kitchen still smelled like her signature meals. I instantly began to salivate just thinking about her pot roast or vegetable beef soup. Her soup was the reason I discovered okra and I still put it in my own soup in honor of her. Her pot roast was beyond good. She always hovered over her electric frying pan holding a fork to test it, one hand on her hip and the other savoring her work. I've tried to make it the same way for many years and even if I put a hand on my own hip while tasting, it still doesn't quite measure up.

What gave Grandma the grandma smell was her morning and evening facial hygiene routine. It involved cold cream, powders and perfume. I remember watching her, in awe of all the time and effort she put into cleaning her face and getting ready for each day. The only makeup she wore was lipstick and powder from a little box with its own applicator pad. She always looked so fresh and smelled so good. I still have a container of her powder on my dresser. Every once in a while, I open it and sniff. Just like that, she's back, laughing at my dad, yelling at her grandkids, and taking care of Grandpa.

Grandpa was blind and had been since I was around one year old. He had been a repair guy for the Alcoa Aluminum Company fixing dairy bottling machines all over the country so he had been a busy boy. A mishap during eye surgery caused him to lose sight in both eyes. His blindness did not stop him from making and fixing things while puttering in his garage shop. There were guide wires strung throughout the property he would use to make his way all over the yard. Anytime we went into his shop, the smell of oil and grease, machinery, tools and projects, was the first thing we noticed. It was the Grandpa smell.

When he was done for the day, he would make his way into the house, first coming to a sink just inside the door where he would wash up, or going into the little bathroom just inside the mudroom door where there was a toilet and little shower. On the last day we were in the house, I wandered into the little bathroom and was overcome with the smell of him. Sweat, grease, and Ivory soap. It was a working man's bathroom that brought him back to life for me. I leaned against the back wall of the shower, slid down and cried. It was a moment I will never forget.

When I was in college, my parents lived down in southern California. I worked a couple jobs during the summer and lived in their house to save money, sharing a bedroom with one of my sisters. My brother, Bruce, had his own room. The door to his bedroom was set up where the top half could swing in and the bottom would still be closed. Reminded me of a horse stall in a stable somewhere and as it turned out, was fitting. He was a marathon runner at the time so he spent a lot of time sweating, most especially his feet. I cannot sufficiently describe the odor of his feet without feeling a little nauseous. There are no words for the stench. If he left his door open, the smell would waft down the hallway, into other parts of the house, including my bedroom. Not good.

One day, I was sitting on the bed in my room. Movement caught my eye and I looked up to see Dad in a crouch, heading down the hall. To this day, I don't know why he was crouching. Maybe it just felt more sneaky. He had something in his hand and motioned me to remain quiet. I got up and tip-toed to the doorway just in time to see him fling open the top part of the door to Bruce's room and begin spraying. Lysol and yelling ensued. Dad stood up and raced back down the hallway in glee. Bruce was sputtering and I was laughing.

Even today, the smell of Lysol, not a pleasant odor in itself, brings me right back to the delight on Dad's face as he raced back to wherever he thought he'd be safe. We had all yelled at Bruce for not washing his feet after a run to no avail but this time he got the not-so-subtle hint and started spraying his shoes and washing his feet after a run. Ah yes, good times. Whenever I get a whiff of stinky feet, I instantly think of my brother, Lysol and Dad. Is that weird?

Liver and onions. Need I say more? Unfortunately, Dad liked it and Mom would cook it. Not very often but when she did, I would start getting the dry heaves and knew I needed to run away. Far, far away. I'd rather eat Bruce's socks.

Whenever I smell an outdoor grill going, I'm transported. And hungry. Dad had an aluminum cast grill on wheels that followed us wherever we moved. He took great care of it, even having it sand-blasted to get it really clean every once in a while. He'd load up the bottom with briquets, build a pyramid with them, squirt it with lighter fluid, and set it on fire. Once the lighter fluid burned off, the heavenly scent of burning charcoal would fill the air. As soon as he threw the hamburgers on, I knew we were in for my favorite meal. I then went into shameless drooling mode. While I savored every bite, I wondered, not for the first time, what was better, the smell or the taste.

Grandpa, Grandma, and Dad are gone. Bruce and his feet are halfway around the world in Thailand. Who knew Lysol, marathon feet, pot roast, machine oil, cold cream, and Grandpa sweat would evoke such sweet memories? One whiff and little movies play out in my head from those times. I love how they always bring a smile to my face.

Every time.

$$\sim\ 6\ \sim$$

NOT A MORNING PERSON

If I had to describe myself in twenty words or less, six of them would be *'I am not a morning person'* and then I'd use the rest to warn everyone. It is a burden I have carried my whole life except when I was a baby. According to my mother, I was a good baby no matter what time of day but I have no recollection of that time. Then again, I was the first child born to our family so of course I was a good baby. The first child is always good and stays that way all her life. She can't help it.

While not a morning person I am an amazing night owl. I love to read and can stay up until the first inkling of sunrise shows on the horizon. Then I freak out and wonder where the time went. I can't tell you how many books I've read lying in bed, reading away and telling myself over and over, *'when I get to the end of this chapter, I'll quit'* and then before I know it, I've finished the book. Self-discipline and a good book are not good friends. They are at war almost every night in my world.

I blame the authors. The really good ones finish off each chapter with temptation, wrought with either a blatant or subtle need to continue to the next chapter. It's the subtle ones I have to watch out for. I may think I can put the book down and go to sleep but after I turn off the light, put on my CPAP mask, find my comfy spot on the pillow, and close my eyes, the end of the chapter nags at my brain. Pretty soon the mask comes off, the light goes on, and the book is in my hands again.

Being a night owl means one of two things: I either sleep in and get up somewhere between nine and noon or I don't get much sleep and need a nap all day long. Either way, it takes time to wake up and be fairly coherent.

I'm not exactly grumpy in the morning. I just need time to get my bearings, find my groove, get the stuff out of my eyes, go to the bathroom, and just breathe. I don't want to answer hard questions like what I'm planning on doing that day or even how well I slept. I need time to wake up. Since I'm not party to morning people's routines, I have no idea if they wake up talking and being active. Have they had coffee and had five minutes to realize they just got out of bed? Was their first thought *'hey, let's go run five miles?'* Did they miss talking for eight hours so they now have to chat about their dreams or plans and other positive stuff? I don't get it. Never have and never will.

Sleeping is the one thing I always thought I was an expert at. When I sleep, I rarely remember my dreams and I never feel the need to share them with anyone when I wake up. It's my gift to those that don't feel like talking in the morning either. I can and have slept through storms, wind, and other people who snore worse than I do, as long as I fall asleep before they do. I don't even notice the dogs and cats who feel the need to surround me while we all sleep. The same goes for lights, the sun, or all the alarms I set to wake me up. Or the people who punch me because I can sleep through those alarms. My sister recently told me she doesn't know how I can sleep through the Led Zeppelin 'Whole Lotta Love' song I have set on my phone or hit the snooze button five times without actually waking.

When I was in college and had roommates, I would often wake up in the morning and notice my bed covered with shoes and books and other things that weren't there when I went to sleep. Apparently, and I have no recollection of this, I snore. The deeper the sleep, the louder I snored, and thus the bigger the pile of things on me or the floor. They threw everything they could find at my inert body in vain attempts to get me to stop snoring. My poor roommates.

Years later, I learned I had sleep apnea. I also learned I could die because of it. I thought it might explain why it was so hard for me to wake up. I wasn't actually sleeping. The fog of each morning could be explained by lack of oxygen. I wonder if I can blame my horrible math skills on sleep apnea.

Sleep apnea was only part of the big picture regarding sleep patterns of my life. Once I got used to wearing a mask and listening to the CPAP machine, I thought maybe I'd wake up with more vim and vigor. Perhaps I could become a morning person. Nope. I just looked scary and sounded like Darth Vader.

Getting up for school or work all of my life before 7am made me feel like the walking dead for most of the morning. There was no bounce to my step or chit chat allowed. I really resented those people who get up and feel the need to talk and be chipper. Happy people in the morning make me want to hurt something. I need quiet and it is not in the nature of morning people to be quiet in the morning. They are ready for the day and feel the need to do horrible things like make big decisions or exercise. What is wrong with them?

My Circadian Rhythm has always been night owl versus early bird. It's almost like being left-handed in a right-handed world. Life favors one over the other. I am left-handed so I know. We don't plan on being left-handed or a night owl, it just happens. And it's almost impossible to change. I know because I have tried. I thought when I retired, I would continue to get up every morning around 7. Nope.

Let's just say it didn't take long to fall into my natural rhythm. Oh, I can get up early if I have to, and without complaint. But I embrace my late nights followed by late mornings without shame. I'm never going to be a morning person no matter what time I get up. My best advice to anyone who tries to engage me before noon is **'Danger, Approach with Caution. Consider Yourself Warned!'**

7

SAVE THE WORMS!!

Even my grandson shares my love of earthworms.
That's my guy!!!

Not many people in this world will freely admit to a long and storied relationship with worms. Various kinds of earthworms to be precise. I don't know why anyone wouldn't consider it as some kind of lifetime achievement. But I do.

For me, it started decades ago when I was in junior high school and our Air Force family was stationed in the Philippines. We lived off base while waiting for base housing to become available. A tropical storm blew in bringing so much rain and wind I thought our house would blow off the foundation and we'd float away. I remember two things about that night. The electricity had gone out and I needed to go to the bathroom. So, I took a lit candle and set it on top of the toilet so I could see while I went about my business. Who pays attention to the towels hanging from the rack above it or that they could catch on fire? I really wasn't trying to burn the house down. The other thing we saw was an undulating mass of giant worms that covered the streets outside. They were bigger than nightcrawlers and they were everywhere, having escaped the saturated soil for higher and drier ground. It was the strangest sight I'd ever seen in my twelve years of living. When the wind finally stopped and the rain was more like a mist, they just disappeared. I've never forgotten the wonder of all those worms. Or the smell of burned towels.

When we got reassigned to another base near Tacoma, Washington a couple years later, we lived near a lake and I learned all about fishing. It was where I discovered the important relationship between worms and fish. I became quite adept at jabbing a fishing hook into a worm several times and launching it out into the lake to lure and catch perch or catfish. If the worm wasn't too beat up from being woven onto the hook and hurled through the air a bunch of times, I could get two or three fish from one worm. That made up for the time it took me to learn to impale it just right to keep it on the hook. There were a few missteps in the beginning where I'd cast and the worm landed a lot farther away than the hook, weights, and bobber. I'd helplessly watch the whole set up land in the water. Beyond it, much further out, another little blip would break the surface of the water and I knew the worm was free and my hook was bare.

I never bought worms for fishing. I found them. I learned their secrets. Moist but not wet soil usually yielded enough worms for an afternoon of feeding the fish. Peeking under rocks or downed logs, I was a worm hunting machine. It was a battle of wills when I'd grab a worm that tried to zip back down into the soil. It stretched and I pulled gently as I waited patiently for it to relax a bit so I could finesse a little of it out of its escape route. Most of the time I won. Sometimes, the worm won. Or, the worm would break in half and I'd feel bad for hurting it. The fact that I used them as bait didn't bother me, but breaking them in half did. I don't get it either.

In college soil courses, I learned the real benefit of worms and I became a worm champion. I somehow found new meaning in the word 'dirt' by embracing the role of the earthworm. I also credit cartoonist, Gary Larsen, who showed worm families living like humans. Who doesn't love worms with lips and eyeglasses, makeup and clothes? I know I do.

Since that time, I give a lot more thought to how I can best serve what I now call *'wormanity.'* Whenever I start a new flower bed or garden plot, I check the worm population by digging up several shovels of dirt to see if I even have any worms. If I don't have any or just a couple, I do worm transplants.

That's how I ended up flashlight diving with friends for night-crawlers for my garden in Utah in the early 1980s.

The thing about nightcrawlers is they are perfectly named and are way bigger in size than regular earthworms. These large beastly worms come out of the ground at night but anchor themselves to *terra firma* in case someone or something tries to get them. If they sense movement, they are back in the ground like spaghetti getting slurped into an eight-year-old boy's mouth.

Stealthy movement, quick reflexes, convincing feints, and superior peripheral vision are a must for obtaining hundreds of the wily nightcrawlers. So, one night we planned our strategy for success. One friend was designated to hold a flashlight in preparation for attack, while the rest of us staged ourselves around the yard. No one moved. There was just enough ambient light to see movement on the ground. As if on some secret worm signal, nightcrawlers emerged from the depths. Still, no one moved. When the night-crawlers got about half way out of the ground, the flashlight came on and the pouncing commenced. We wrestled with nightcrawlers like crazed maniacs from a science fiction movie. If someone was really good, they would have a nightcrawler in each hand, grinning like a fool.

As the night went on, we filled an entire coffee can with night-crawlers. We, the people, felt victorious. I took my new worker worms out to the garden where I had lovingly prepared their new homes. The soil in my garden was not great for much besides weeds but I was determined to have vegetables. Before I released them, I gave them a pep talk about their new world, new job, and the importance of each and every one of them. I'm sure it was inspiring. I then thanked them for what they would bring to the health of our world and the future success of my garden. I doubt any worm has heard that kind of thing before. I don't know why because they should. It's always important to express gratitude.

Every once in a while, I think back on those days and wish someone would have videoed us. I'm not sure if it would be looked at as some kind of weird orgy where no one touches another person, or some freakishly incomprehensible horror movie. I just know it would be dang funny.

These days, whenever it rains, you can find me outside, bent over, trying to pick up the worms that seem to think the pavement or sidewalk is a better place to be. It is not easy to pick up worms on pavement. It has taken some time to get the hang of it but I think I've got it down. I'll usually make the worm mad by stopping its progress. As it contorts, I grab it. If it doesn't contort, I tickle its tail. I've gotten to be pretty adept. Once I have a handful, I find a place that's not as wet in the vegetation and set them free. I tell them goodbye and good luck, and then wipe my hands on my pants.

Be safe my little slimy friends. And thanks for all you do to make our world a better place.

8

BOLO FOR MY PASSPORT

Passport photo-Age 12
Haven't had a passport picture this good since.

BOLO: Be-On-The-Lookout for my secret place. If you find it, you will be amazed at all the things in there. My secret place(s), over time, have become this black hole in the universe and my life. Since I insist on placing items in a safe and secret place it's my own fault. When will I learn?

When I retired, I decided to renew my passport so I could go visit my brother who, at the time, was working in South Africa. I went to Costco and got my new passport picture taken. Next, I began the search for my birth certificate. It was in an old secret place. Could I remember where that was? No. I looked everywhere. Many, many times. I sent away for a new one from the county where I was born so long ago. Luckily, they don't keep important things in secret places and I received a new birth certificate in a timely manner.

I had found my old long expired passport so I could complete the form and send it all in. Guess where that was. I had run across it while looking for my birth certificate. It had been safely tucked away in my sock drawer, the most obvious secret place ever besides the underwear drawer. Feeling like I had things under control, I mailed off all the necessary documentation and received my new passport sooner than I expected.

What did I do with it? I immediately put it and my newly acquired birth certificate in a new secret place because these are very important kinds of documents and I hadn't yet decided when I would go visit my brother. I wasn't totally committed about visiting South Africa because of all the horror stories he had told me and I waffled for a long time about when I would go. By the time he finally talked me into visiting, the location of the secret place housing my new passport was gone from my brain.

The sad thing about all this was the missed opportunity to go see him there because after a couple of years he moved to Thailand. In the meantime, my sister went over to South Africa and had a great time. I blame myself. Mostly I blame myself for finding a secret place that seemed so obvious at the time. Why wasn't it obvious when I needed it?

The good news was that while searching for one secret place, I found other secret places containing birthday presents for various family members I had hidden years ago. Like a lot of years ago. Unfortunately, the latest Barbie doll with tiny plastic ski boots and skis, is no longer relevant to my now 25- year-old daughter. Or the Fisher Price tub set with floating frogs, ducks, and fish, made for kids less than 3 years old which would not be well received by my now 10-year-old grandson who only takes showers. I am beyond heavy sighing.

I did find two packages of Hershey's chocolate covered marsh-mallow Easter eggs. These delightful treats only come out around Easter so they are always a precious commodity. I don't share them with anyone so I hide them really well. These were really old and the chocolate had gone from luscious to faded yucky brown. The marshmallow part was solid, impossible to take a bite out of. Yes, I tried to eat it. Even my rock hammer barely made a dent in one. I found a dozen now petrified eggs that went directly to the garbage. This was a missed opportunity I regret to this day.

Back to the sad passport story. I decided to apply for another passport, thinking if I get another new one, I'd find the old new one. It would just magically appear because that's how this kind of thing works.

I took my extra passport pictures from the previous effort, got another copy of my birth certificate, filled out the application again and went down to the post office to send it all off again. That's when I found out the rules for the pictures had changed and they didn't allow people to wear glasses anymore. Back to Costco I went to get more pictures taken without my glasses. It felt like some kind of miracle when I got it sent off.

When the new passport showed up, I did not find a secret place for it. I told everyone in my family where I had put it so when I asked later, someone could tell me where it was. For an entire month I walked over to the place I had put it so it was ingrained in my brain. No way was I losing this sucker again.

I've now used my new passport three times and I'm so afraid of losing it while on these trips, I sleep with it. When I get home from a trip, I don't stop to pet the dogs or cats who I haven't seen for weeks. I make a beeline to the place my passport resides and carefully put it there. Then I breathe and commence to revel in the joy of my furry kids, surreptitiously glancing up at my passport to make sure it hasn't disappeared into thin air.

I still haven't run across my old new passport. I keep expecting to. It is possible it will never appear in my lifetime but I hope it does. I really, really want to know where it's been all this time even if I can't use it. It's driving me a little bit crazy. I know it wasn't stolen because it's in a secret place. The best one ever.

Anyone need a Barbie with boots and skis in the original packaging? The tub toys are really fun but I'm keeping them. So there.

~ 9 ~

FOR THE LOVE OF PUPPIES

The lucky 7. It was all worth it.
Just wish I could have kept one. Or all.

Early 2018

It has been four weeks since a lot of lives changed in an instant. At the moment, I am sitting in my writing chair, alternately typing and letting my eyes rest on three sleeping puppies and thinking about how quickly the priorities of my life have been altered. I've finally had a good night's sleep and my mind is clear. The melding of unrelated events once again reminds me of the resilience of both people and animals in heartwarming and heartbreaking ways.

A few months ago, my friend Diane brought her female Corgi, Priscilla Jane, over to my house to breed with my male Corgi, Tank. Diane had been planning this for some time. She had waited through the heat cycle that seems to last forever in un-spayed female dogs and it was finally time. We let the two of them outside to get acquainted thinking it might take a while. Diane had even brought an overnight bag and bed for Priscilla in case she needed to stay a while. To say Priscilla Jane was ready is an understatement. Tank, still a puppy himself, wanted to play but when she wouldn't, he took one sniff and proceeded to 'do the deed.'

Diane and I sat at the dining room table over cups of coffee, trying not to check out the action while attempting meaningful conversation. We finally breathed a sigh of relief when both dogs, now disengaged, came to the sliding glass door to be let in. Tank and I thought our jobs were done. I had provided the intact male dog and Tank had provided the means for the possibility of puppies. It was up to Priscilla Jane now.

A month went by and we wondered if Priscilla Jane was pregnant because she showed no signs that were obvious to either of us. Diane later commented that she thought Priscilla Jane had morning sickness and seemed more lethargic during the day. Really? I guess she would know since they live together.

Two weeks later Diane took Priscilla Jane in for an ultrasound and lo and behold, five puppies showed up on the screen. We gave each other a high five and went back to our respective homes. I told Tank the good news while I packed for a three-week trip to Thailand to see my brother Bruce and his family. When my sister and I had booked this trip, about six months prior to all this seemingly unrelated activity, I thought the only challenges ahead of me were enduring the heat of Thailand and keeping up with my 8- year-old niece. Boy, was I wrong.

Off I went on my merry way about ten days before the due date. I stayed in touch with Diane through emails and texts. The day before we left on a little side trip to Laos, I got an email from Diane saying that Priscilla Jane had had 13 puppies and had died during the C-section. My heart stopped. I felt sick, sad, and totally helpless. There was nothing I could do but wait until the time difference between Thailand and Montana was reasonable for a call.

When I finally reached Diane, I found out more of the details and the current situation. Four of the puppies had died. She was home with the nine newborn puppies to feed and care for. I couldn't imagine her grief and pain or doing all of that by herself. I didn't know how to change my flight plans from a foreign country so I just tried to support her from afar.

Fortunately, several former coworkers from our Forest Service office stepped up and began going out to Diane's house to help feed and provide relief and companionship to all. Other friends and family helped out. One thing that never ceases to amaze and humble me is how, in the darkest of times, the very best in people comes pouring forth like a wave of warmth. It's sincere, genuine and very much appreciated, especially when you are so exhausted you don't even know your own name.

Meanwhile, I had reached the point in the trip when I was ready to get home so when the time came, I could hardly wait. I wanted to see my home, my furry family, and the puppies. Of course, my trip home from Thailand turned out to be filled with all kinds of drama and trauma. We made the leg from Phuket to Bangkok with no problems. When we checked into our next flight, my sister got her ticket and I was told that I didn't have a ticket. What? In halting English, I was told to call Delta Airlines to find out what happened. I went off to the quietest place I could find in the airport and called the number on my itinerary. After listening to a mechanical voice, I was sent to reservations where I was told to expect my wait to be 2 hours until an agent would be available. My plane was supposed to leave in 2 hours but I hung on. At exactly 30 minutes, the line went dead.

I went back to the check in line to see if I could talk to a supervisor for help. When I finally got in front of him, I handed him my paper itinerary and told him I needed help. He did a bunch of typing and showed me the screen. It said that I had an open ticket. What does that even mean? I was beyond confused and frustrated but I stayed calm. I offered to buy a new ticket and he said that would only get me to Shanghai, China, not to the U.S. I told my sister to go without me. Good thing she loves me because she didn't. I knew I liked her for a reason.

He got on the phone and spent a lot of time talking in Thai to someone who must've found a way to get past this glitch. My hopes for a positive resolution went up and down with the expressions on his face. Finally, my supervisor guy told me to go down to the next check in counter. He handed a piece of paper to the woman there who typed some things in and then handed me a boarding pass. He told me I'd have to get the next boarding pass in China. I was so relieved and grateful, I hugged everyone within reach.

Side note-we got to see supervisor guy get an award for what we thought was customer service. I clapped really loud. No matter what he got it for I think he deserved one for dealing with the Delta Airlines reservation system.

After going through several security lines, we got to the gate and immediately boarded the plane. The doors shut, the plane backed out and then stopped. We sat there for almost an hour. The engines would rev up and then down. The captain came on and said something was wrong with one of the engines and we would have to de-board the plane. Buses came out to take us back to the terminal. The doors did not open and we continued to sit. It got really warm in the plane and the guy behind me was starting to panic saying he was claustrophobic. Then the buses went away. As we sat, I thought about how it would feel to punch that guy behind me in the head. Dude, no one is happy about this.

Then the captain came back on to tell us that the engine was fine and we were leaving. This news made everyone nervous, especially my sister, who thought the engine would fall off the plane in flight. I told her I'd watch and let her know when it did. For some reason, this did not comfort her. I had said it calmly. What more could she want?

We got to the Pudong airport outside of Shanghai a bit late but all the engines had stayed on and functional so it was hard to complain. We still had 2 hours until our next flight left. Since I didn't have a boarding pass, I realized I didn't know how I was going to get through security. Fortunately, there was a man from the airlines waiting just outside the entrance to security. He ran up and handed me my pass. I must've looked desperate so I was easy to recognize.

But Chinese security was not done with me. I had to have my picture taken, hand over my previous boarding pass, new boarding pass, passport, and as he typed on his computer, the security guy kept looking at me like I was going to pull a gun or something. It was disconcerting. Meanwhile, my sister was scowling at me like it was all my fault.

The 11-hour leg of the flight from China to Los Angeles was the one that kicked my butt. Being incredibly smart, I had gotten Economy Comfort for the long leg of the trip so I had more leg room and supposedly, more seat room. I didn't factor in the possibility that I'd be sitting next to a large man who snored. He spilled over the arm rest and I found myself hugging the window and wearing earplugs. We finally got to Salt Lake City and to sister Tracey's house just before midnight. It's hard to sleep when you know you have to because you have an eight hour drive the next day. All I could think about was seeing the puppies. And, oh yeah, checking on poor Diane who was undoubtedly as exhausted as I was.

I don't remember much about the drive home. I just drove. When I got to Diane's, I was overcome with more emotions than I knew I had been holding onto. One look at Diane and I knew she was running on fumes. The puppies were beyond adorable and for some reason, bigger than I had imagined. How had they all fit inside Priscilla Jane? I couldn't believe all the colors and markings or the tiny little noses and feet and ears. I was smitten and terrified.

Already, the puppies, now ten days old, were writhing in puppy dreams as they slept. What do puppies who can't see or hear have dreams about?

Diane then told me the whole story of the day they were born. I could tell it weighed heavily on her and she had not had any time to grieve the loss of her Priscilla Jane. As with any kind of tragedy, there was a lot of second guessing, guilt and anguish. And for about the millionth time, I felt helpless. What do you say?

I knew the best help I could offer was to just be there. As the puppies began to wake up and demand more formula, I held each one and marveled at their features and spirits. So soft, so little, so vulnerable, so dependent on us. It was almost overwhelming. I say almost because I was in a fog. Jet lag, lack of restful sleep, and the emotions of the past 36 hours led me to an almost catatonic state.

I went home, promising Diane I would be back first thing in the morning to help and come up with a plan. I pulled into the garage, went into the house and found myself sitting on the floor in the kitchen, surrounded by my two Corgis, Maizy and Tank. There was a lot of wiggling and wet kisses. My heart was happy and full. My two kitties joined the fray and I realized once again that one of the best things about traveling is coming home.

For the next several weeks, Diane and I tried a couple different strategies designed to get both of us some real sleep and keep up with the feeding and cleaning schedule. With that many puppies, feeding one puppy at a time it took the better part of 90 minutes. The cacophony of nine hungry puppies was intense but as each one was fed, it died down to the sound of contented bliss. Once all were asleep, the cleanup process began. Bottles were rinsed out, the towels used in their box were removed and thrown into the laundry. What seemed like only minutes later, one puppy would wake up and demand more food which would wake up the others and the whole process started again.

Even with the exhaustion, tears and stress of it all, we had a lot of moments where cuteness and tenderness took over. These were puppies after all so how could we not love them? One of the fun things about having them all together was watching their interactions with us and each other. We started to name them. The four boys became Sherman, Big Bear, Bolt, and Clark. I personally named Clark because when he ate, he stretched out like Superman. When he was done, he was the unassuming Clark Kent. Sherman was named for his dad Tank. Big Bear had a sister named Little Bear. They were twins in coloring and demeanor. Bolt was a big boy with the coolest jagged stripe from his nose to the back of his neck. The girl's names evolved over time. The two tri-colored girls were first called the Twisted Sisters because they wanted to nurse on the male puppy boy parts. They later became Scout and Scooter. Mattie got her name from me and I don't know why I came up with it, it just seemed to fit. Angel was just that. She was just sweet all the time which meant she got picked on but didn't fight back. She was also incredibly adorable.

Our first strategy was for one of us to have all the puppies for two days while the other person slept and caught up with real life. We were hauling all the puppies from one house to the other every other day. The trouble began when two of the puppies got pneumonia after aspirating formula. They cried piteously for hours and it was gut wrenching. Trips to the vet and antibiotics didn't save them and we lost them. When we said goodbye to Big Bear and Bolt, it was like losing a part of our hearts.

It didn't take more than a week before we changed to the final new strategy. We divided and conquered. I took Scout, Scooter and Mattie. Diane got Sherman, Little Bear, Angel and Clark.

The next few weeks were just as consuming but without the fear and frantic pace. Life settled down to more regular sleep, routine training, and feeding. Once they could eat real food, feeding time became pure entertainment for me. I'd mix warm formula and baby cereal with dry puppy food and make a mush. Then I'd put it on a paper plate, set it on the floor and watch the chaos. Three puppies, each with their front paws holding down the plate, all pushing toward the middle, eating like there was no tomorrow. When it was all gone, they would stagger away like they were drunk. I'd clean their little faces and put them into the little kid swimming pool where they'd snuggle down for a nap.

As soon as I heard them stir, I'd pick them up and run them outside and tell them to go potty. Within a minute, all three would go. I'd tell them what good little puppies they were and cuddle for a bit with each of them. It was our happy time. Since it was spring, I pulled out some of my gardening tools and pretended to get some work done with all my new little helpers. Mostly, I took pictures and just watched them explore their new world and each other. Puppy fights are all noise and uncoordinated wrestling.

And what did Tank and Maizy think about all this? One of the most extraordinary things was how Tank took over some of the mom duties. He would follow a puppy around and use his nose to lift up their rear ends. Within seconds, the puppy would poop. Unfortunately, he sometimes cleaned up after them which made me gag a little bit. He did this parenting thing from the time I brought them home until they were about six weeks old. It was so sweet.

As the puppies got more mobile, Maizy got more interested in them. She's kind of a nervous little dog so when they started following her around the yard, she'd snap at them. They didn't care. After a bit, she'd try to get them to play with her. And when they settled down to nap in the grass, she would lie down near them and keep an eye on things.

We didn't have any trouble finding the perfect homes for them. For me, the trouble came when it was time to let them go. Each little personality had become a part of my heart. Oh, I knew better than to get attached but how is it possible not to? I have no idea. It's part of my DNA to love animals more than quite honestly, most people. I would have given my right arm to keep them all, but two dogs and two cats were enough. Five dogs and two cats might have been a little much. After all, I only have two hands and it's already hard when everyone wants attention at the same time.

As each puppy went off to their forever homes, my heart really hurt. But they all went off to terrific homes with people who would love them as much as I did. That made it a bit more tolerable. Mattie stayed local and has two little boys to keep her in line. Scooter went off to Alaska and is living the life with her new mom and grandma. Scout went on a long road trip to Albuquerque, New Mexico, where she is learning to be bilingual. Kidding.

I hear from them all. Well, I hear from their moms. I get pictures and reports. I'm hoping to see them in person someday just to see if they remember me at all. I know I'll never forget them.

In hindsight I realize I had made a lot of assumptions about my role in this whole dog breeding thing. As Tank and I discussed, his role before we even got started was obvious. I thought mine was to provide him and that would be it. I'm sure if things had progressed the way they were supposed to it would have been true. I would have watched from afar as the puppies grew up with their mother who fed and cleaned them until it was time to go to their new homes. It was all just another fine example of how we plan and God laughs.

And as for Diane, the next time she has another brilliant idea I will pat her on the head, say a very firm 'NO!', and walk away.

Scout and Scooter, aka The Twisted Sisters

~ 10 ~

JOB OF A LIFETIME PART 1

You just never know what kinds of jobs you will end up doing when you sign on with the state doing a bunch of ongoing research studies. My introduction to work at Hardware Ranch near Logan, Utah involved weighing and tagging elk calves right after they were born. No babies were hurt. Confused, yes. Hurt, no. We were quick so their moms wouldn't decide to hurt us. Except for one mom who kept us on our toes.

This is a preamble to the career part of my life. Going to college was non-negotiable in my family. I tried really hard to pick a major and after three years managed to stumble into a class in Range Science, something I'd never heard of. For some reason, it spoke to me and as I learned about the great outdoors in terms of plants, water, soils, wildlife, ecology and livestock, I knew I'd found my calling. I don't know why it clicked, it just did and I'm forever grateful. This first story is about the temporary jobs I had during the college years that gave me some of the skills I would need in the future.

For the longest time, I've been trying to figure out how to explain my career in a way that makes sense, isn't too technical or oversimplified and is not patronizing. The problem is, unless you are a rancher or a fellow worker in my field, you probably won't know what the heck I'm talking about.

In 1979, I graduated from college with a B.S. degree in Range Science. The B.S. is going to be flowing now but the degree is real science stuff. It has to do with understanding and working on rangelands covered mostly in grass or shrubs that are used for livestock grazing or other forage-eating critters. The classes I took were mainly about plant identification (*what exactly is that plant?*), wildlife habitats (*what is eating these plants or hanging out here, there and everywhere that is not a cow, sheep or horse*), soil classification (*dig a deep pit and see a layered profile of soils not as interesting to most normal people as a Facebook profile*), hydrology (*is there anything more important than water?*), statistics (*yeah, I sucked at that part*), chemistry (*yup, soils and plants have great chemistry together*), economics (*I sucked at that too*), and a few other things like zoology, ecology, and plant physiology.

During the summers and falls of my college education, I worked seasonally, doing some pretty weird stuff. Through the Utah State University Extension, I worked for the Utah Division of Wildlife Resources (DWR) helping collect data for a bunch of different research studies. One summer, I lived in a travel trailer parked out at Hardware Ranch, near Logan, Utah. The main purpose of the ranch was to feed elk in the winter. The ranch workers cut hay in the summer to feed them. There were horses, elk, and peacocks. Several different long term research studies were carried out on the ranch and I got to participate in many of them. I had no idea what I was in for.

One of the studies had to do with keeping about 15 cow elk from the wintering herd in an enclosure in the spring. Once the cow elk gave birth, three of us would drive up close to the calf, jump out of our truck, grab, weigh, and tag the calf really fast. It was no surprise the mom elk didn't want us anywhere near their newborn babies. Can't blame them and we couldn't exactly explain to them what we were doing so they wouldn't worry. Once all the cow elk gave birth, they were set free.

There was this one cow elk who had only one eye thus her not very creative name One-Eyed-Cow. We had to keep our eyes on her whenever we drove in to weigh any calf. She'd get mad and stalk us. When *her calf* was born, we knew she was going to have to be distracted or one or all three of us could get seriously injured. When the birth finally happened, I was chosen to drive while the other two technicians got out and snuck alongside the moving truck. I managed to drive in between her and her baby while they weighed and tagged it. All three of us were already in mega heart pounding mode, but when she jumped up on the hood of the truck to get to her baby, we all freaked out. Ever had a one-eyed cow elk look at you through the windshield with hate in her eye as she slid across the hood? I can still see it today.

It was a good thing the truck was an old beater already or it would have been hard to explain to an insurance person what happened to the hood. I was never so glad as when the last cow gave birth and we were able to open the gates and let them all out because the one-eyed cow chased us every time we went in the enclosure. The really odd thing was that, once allowed to go back into the wild she did not leave. I bet she's still there. It would be just like her to live 50 years.

For some reason I don't remember now, there were two bull elk in another enclosure. I named them Bruce and Norman and spent a lot of time standing at the fence talking to them. Bruce was a big guy and way more friendly than Norman. He spent his days happily eating without worrying about predators. We talked a lot about that as I fed him different grasses through the fence. It felt like we were communicating and usually when I was done with my work for the day, I'd wander down and chat with the boys. They were way nicer than One-Eyed-Cow who sent her evil stare my way from a distance.

The resident male peacock thought my trailer was his throne where he could jump up on top to survey his kingdom and chat loudly to the females of the flock. They mostly ignored him. He seemed to sense when I was inside the trailer because he would jump on top of it, making it sound like the roof was caving in. Even though I knew he was going to do it, it scared me half to death every time. I would go outside and yell at him. He mostly ignored me. What's the deal with peacocks?

One week, I was sent to a remote study area in another mountain range nearby for a few days. My job was to follow two tame deer around in the woods and record what they were doing every 15 minutes. I was told they were famous deer because they had been in an Olympia beer commercial. The job would have been a lot more fun if the deer had brought beer. They didn't.

In addition to using my developing observational skills, I also collected data on several weird things having to do with biting insects. I had to carry around a beach ball that had been spray painted black and count and record how many deer flies and horseflies landed on it every 15 minutes. The deer had been outfitted with monitoring devices to record their heart rates. The purpose of the study was to get information on animal stress caused by these mean flies.

If you haven't been bitten by either the horse or deer fly in your life, consider yourself lucky. It HURTS! I ended up having to wear a rainsuit with a face shield to keep from being wounded. The poor deer had no chance. Their ears and tails were in constant motion. I'm guessing we all had elevated heart rates and blood loss during different times throughout the 24-hour periods.

When the summer ended, I had racked up a lot of experiences I'll never forget. I also ended up with mononucleosis and faced a brutal schedule back at school. All I remember about it was sleeping a lot and dropping classes and my GPA.

For three years during the school year, I got to work at a deer check station. Students were hired during big game hunting season to gather data from hunters about where they hunted and, if they were successful, remove a tooth from the deer. This was done to age the deer population in each hunting district. We set up in Spanish Fork canyon where Highway 6 runs through so a lot of hunters from many areas of Utah were stopped and questioned. The men who worked for DWR oversaw the whole operation from teaching us how to easily remove a tooth from a deer and how to direct traffic.

It was fun. We got to talk to lots of people about their hunt. Hunters like to tell war stories and we were good listeners. When we had to take a tooth the comments from the hunters generally went something like *'Are you in dental school?'* or *'I wouldn't want you for my dentist.'* I always pretended they were funny and acted like I hadn't heard that a gazillion times before.

One year, I was working my lane of traffic when an old station wagon with an older man pulled up. I began my standard *How was your hunt?'* routine when I looked up on top of his car and noticed he didn't have a deer up there, he had a burro. There are wild burros in Utah and he had bagged one. I didn't know what to do so I called out to one of the game wardens to come over and see what we had. The man really thought he had a deer. The warden and I looked at each other and he made a decision to let him keep it. He obviously needed the meat. Then the hunter asked me if I was going to take a tooth. I did.

As previously mentioned, I somehow managed to graduate with a range science degree along with minors in botany and chemistry. I have no idea how it happened because it was down to the wire in passing my statistics final but it was a relief to finally be done. I'm pretty sure the minor in chemistry was from taking enough chemistry classes other than organic to meet the requirement. Five years of college and I was ready for a steady paycheck. Unfortunately, there weren't any permanent jobs at the time so I looked for a seasonal job.

I found one working for the Bureau of Land Management in Worland, Wyoming. The agency hired about 40 people from colleges all over the country to help do an inventory of the vegetation over about a million acres in this one area called Grass Creek, near a place called Hamilton Dome. Talk about middle of nowhere. They put us up in an elementary school located in an oilfield so we were surrounded by those pumps that look like tipping up and down dinosaurs. The guys were in one classroom and the women in another. Little beds filled up each classroom. It felt like we were in the military. We ate in the cafeteria overseen by two of the nicest people ever. The food was fantastic and before we'd head out for the day, they'd hand us our lunch bags with a smile. It felt like we were headed off for school each day.

In order to get us to and from our scattered inventory areas, we were provided with a fleet of about 20 four-wheel drive Jeep Wagoneers and one older International pickup we called the Rhino. Back in those days, most vehicles had manual transmissions. Only about half of the people knew how to drive one and it was a miracle the transmissions made it through the summer. Teaching someone to drive a stick shift is not for the faint of heart. It required patience and a neck brace. Every stop we had to make had me yelling at my partner *'PUSH IN THE CLUTCH!!!'* Reminding someone to shift while the RPMs topped out at 6,000 was pretty normal. Yelling over the sound of the screaming engine was not.

We worked in teams of two. Every day, each team was handed aerial photographs marked up with Xs for where we were to run transects. Each team also had a big hoop, like the hula kind only made of steel. We'd gather up our equipment and head out. When we'd get to X marks the spot, we'd get to work. One of us would read the data within the hula hoop plots and one would fill out the forms. The hoop was laid down ten times along a distance of anywhere from 100 feet to 100 yards. We weighed and measured everything in it, identifying every plant inside the hoop. We completed the plot by walking around the outside of it counting poop, any kind of poop there was; cow, deer, antelope, horse, elk. It was a very hot summer, the job became very tedious, and there were a lot of bugs. I whined both out loud and in my head. It didn't help.

We were periodically subjected to nasty little gnats called no-seeums that think eyelids are delicious. We could always tell who was in areas with these bloodsucking creatures. Swollen eyes from crying have nothing on no-seeum eyes. And itch! Some of us resorted to smoking cigars in those areas. While the smoke minimized the bugs, the smell and taste in the heat was nauseating. Good times.

One of the best weeks during that summer was when we were taken to remote areas by helicopter. Trying to fit the hula hoop in a Jet Ranger helicopter was a bit problematic but we managed. Our pilot had flown in Vietnam and he was fun and amazing. We swooped over badlands, chased wild horses, and saw everything from new and beautiful perspectives. I did not vomit once. He'd drop us off and tell us he'd see us in a week while laughing maniacally. Fortunately, he came back in the late afternoon to get us in time for supper. Some people didn't take to it like I did and didn't really want supper. Wimps.

At the end of the summer, everyone went back to school. Since I had managed to graduate, I continued my search for a permanent job. In the meantime, I stuck around for the paperwork part of the job, entering the data we had spent all summer collecting. It was my first taste of the boring parts of the project. It was good preparation for my career; managing data and writing reports.

Just as I was finishing up, I got a notice for an interview for a permanent job with the Forest Service in Vernal, Utah. Real life was about to happen and while nervous, I was pretty excited.

Little did I know, the job, when I got it, was the beginning of a mostly beautiful relationship. And it lasted for over 30 years, but that will be a few stories for another time. I promise.

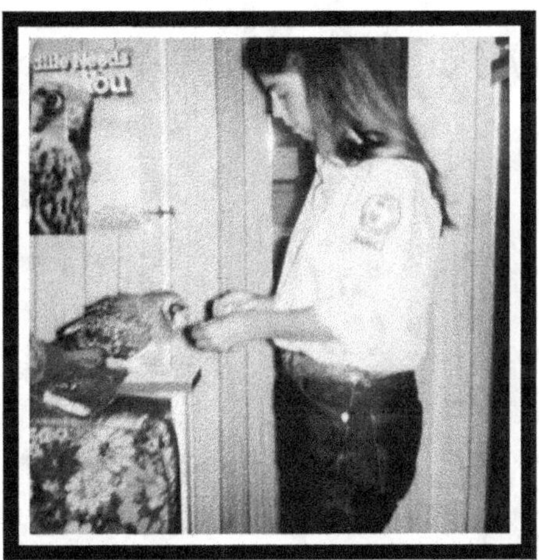

One of the perks of my job with the state was rehabilitating this young short eared owl. I named him Fletcher and he lived in my trailer with me. During the day, he hung outside waiting for me to come home and feed him dead fish or gophers, not my favorite job. When he finally learned to fly and land without giving me a heart attack, he left. I heard he hung around the ranch for several years doing his own gopher and mouse hunting. I've never forgotten him.

~ 11 ~

ARCHAEOLOGY OF THE GARAGE

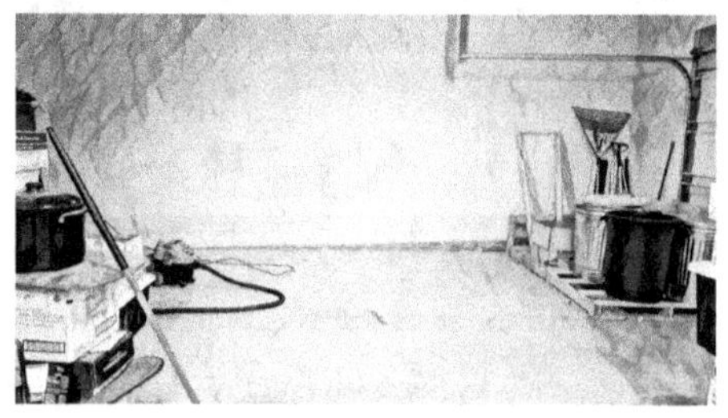

Before-Making room for the makeover.

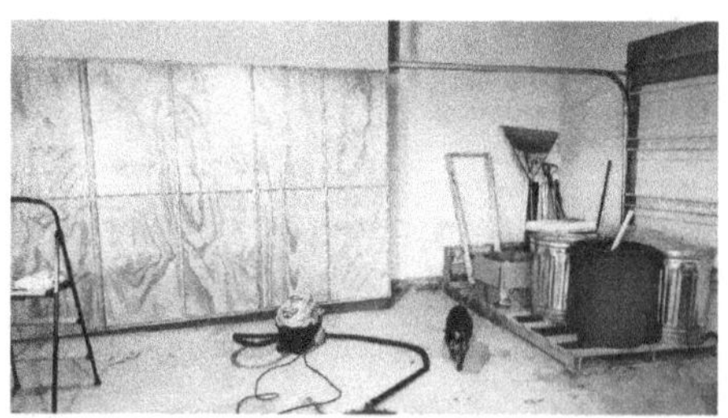

After-Progress Inspector Joseph

The house I live in isn't mine. It belongs to my brother, who at one time, co-owned it with our parents. It has the belongings of three families. I've tried to make it mine but after almost ten years, there still isn't a room that doesn't have something reflecting my brother or our parents. I've tried to understand my hesitation to box up their things and put them somewhere but all I've come up with are excuses. I'm good at excuses. And procrastination. And getting distracted.

The garage is where I've moved some of the things just to get them out of the house. It has reached the point where I can park my truck in there but can't open the door. It's time to do something.

The first hard thing is where to start. Do I start at the top and work my way down? Should I start on the left and work to the right? Maybe I should move everything to the middle and redistribute. I can easily waste a lot of time thinking about this. Finally, I decide to tackle the left side and then work my way around the whole perimeter. Making that decision was exhausting. Is it time for a nap yet?

I grab a garbage can and drag it across the floor to the work bench. The bench is piled high with things I have taken out of my truck and dumped there because I didn't know what to do with them. Layers upon layers, defined by seasons of the year or months of my life are piled high. There isn't a single bit of the actual work bench visible.

Three hours later I've managed to unearth a treasure trove of things I didn't know I had. Granted, some of it belonged to our parents and my brother but most of it was mine. The garbage can is almost full and the work bench actually looks like a work bench. The garage floor, on the other hand, is covered with piles. Piles of old magazines and newspapers or junk mail, rocks, tools, paint, garden seeds and clippers, two of Dad's old toolboxes with nothing much in them, fertilizers and weed killer bottles, and the list goes on. I don't know how many times I said to myself '*I wondered where that went*'; now I know.

I spend the next several hours shuffling the piles to the places they belong. Rocks to the flower beds where I will spend time later finding the right homes for them. The paper pile goes into the house and is dumped unceremoniously next to other piles of paper I need to go through. All the garden stuff is put under the work bench in its own new niche. I open the toolboxes and go through what was left in them, wondering why Dad kept this or that since it was clearly destined to go into the garbage. I can hear him telling me not to throw anything away because I might need it; an almost empty roll of electrical tape, or the stick with a bunch of string wrapped around it, or the random greasy washer, nut or bolt. Just because he grew up in the Depression, doesn't mean I have to save this stuff. Sorry Pop.

That done, I look at my watch and survey the rest of the garage. Why did I think I could get this done in a day? Where will I put any of this except in neat piles along the walls again? I needed a better plan.

After doing a thorough cost analysis involving no actual numbers, I decide to get someone to build some cabinets that are mouse proof and sturdy so I can jam them full of just about everything I could see. I am a big fan of out of sight, out of mind. This part of the plan fits in nicely with my tendency to procrastinate because I would have to wait until the cabinets were built and installed to effectively and efficiently organize the garage. I got them ordered and walked away. Now I could take my nap. Yay!

Towards the end of winter, the cabinets were delivered and installed. They were things of beauty and gave me hope my garage would someday be functional. Because I was anxious to get the ball rolling, I donned winter gear, backed the truck out, closed the garage door, and started sorting things.

As I went through the piles of stuff, I realized there are some things that don't fit into any category. Some belonged to our parents, some were my brother's, and the rest were mine. What to do, what to do? My brain was starting to hurt. My hands and feet were cold. Unexpectedly, I found myself paralyzed by indecision so I dumped each of their piles into boxes, labeled them, and put them on top of the cabinets. Out of reach, out of mind yet again. Whew.

I took the pile of my stuff that didn't fit into any category and threw it into a set of cabinets I like to call 'Miscellaneous Crap.' It's extremely full. Months later, do I know what's in there? Sort of. But if I ever find the screws to the lower panels of the dishwasher, I'll know where the panels are! Or if I decide to cook some kind of Asian food, I can go right to the cabinet and pull out the giant wok that won't fit in any of the kitchen cabinets. Where did it even come from?

Needless to say, I didn't do anything with the cabinets for months. Life got in the way and every time I squeezed my truck into the garage, I was reminded of the need to tackle it again and just get it done.

In the spring a couple of friends who live a few hours away came to visit. Whenever I go over to visit them, they put me to work. Conversely, when they come to visit, they also put me to work. We get a lot of work done whether I want to or not. This time they took one look at the garage and, with scary gleams in their eyes, decided to tackle it. (For the purpose of this story and to maintain their anonymity and so no one tries to steal them, I will call them Wilma and Betty.)

Wilma and Betty tag team me.

Shel, where do you want to all these yard tools to go?
Shel, what's in these boxes?
Shel, do you have any ideas which cabinets to use for certain things?
Shel, what are these?
Shel, what do you want to do with those?

It's a staccato machine gun firing of questions where I am forced to make decisions in nanoseconds or lose the opportunity to have a say. I often panic. The word 'um' comes out of my mouth more often as the day progresses. I go one direction to answer or deal with something Wilma asks and just as quickly, do a lovely pirouette to answer or do something for Betty. There were several moments when I suddenly stopped and stared into space mumbling incoherently. When that happened, Betty would go into the house and bring us glasses of water and make us sit down.

Wilma fidgets. She's on a roll. She's still holding on to the push broom, ready to pounce on the garage floor where layers of mud from the spring mud season are calling to her. Finally, when she gets permission to go back to work, a cloud of dirt dust envelopes us immediately. For that extra caked on mud, she finds a pickax and breaks up the clods while I sweep them into the dustpan and chuck it all outside. What else are you going to do with dirt, put it in the garbage? No, it's going back out in the world where it will probably blow back in someday.

Betty sits down with the label maker and assigns names to cabinets so I'm not opening them all before finding the right one to put something away. As they continue to crack the whip with me, I am starting to feel like my truck really will fit in here again. I'll even be able to open the doors to get in and out of it without hitting something.

Between the layers of dirt and dust, the boxes of stuff belonging to the various household members, and the tools that every garage needs to manage the life inside and outside the house, I feel a sense of order and peace and gratitude. Everything is in its place, out of sight, but now, and most importantly, it will all be easier to find.

I, however, will not be easy to find because I'm going to sneak out to my trailer and take a nap before Wilma and Betty find something else to make me do.

Every once in a while, I go in the garage to get something and stop. My eyes roam around the space and catch a labeled box. It might say 'Mom and Dad, Pine Grove'. The memories of one of the places they lived and my visits there flood my brain. Or I see Dad's toolboxes and think of him working on some project, rummaging around in one, trying to find something. I pull out the foldup chair and sit down. I've long since forgotten why I went in there in the first place but it doesn't matter.

The garage holds parts of my family and my history in layers of time, some decades old and others much more recent. All are precious to me.

I wonder if I can get Wilma and Betty to come back to work on something else like my pantry. Only one person can fit in there at a time and it shouldn't be me.

This is sort of a before shot of part of the garage. We actually began organizing and made paths. Paths are very important. Piles of stuff are very important too. Anybody need anything? I know where it is.

~ 12 ~

MOSQUITOES SUCK

It is dark outside and I am in bed reading before closing my eyes for the night. On one side of me is a sleeping little Corgi named Maizy and on the other side is a badminton racquet looking thing. A mosquito comes at me like I am the meal ticket from nirvana. It buzzes around my head, near my ear, and then my hair before landing on my arm. I have a choice. I can hit it with my hand or I can pick up the racquet, push a button, wave it in the general direction of the mosquito who spooked at my movement. **ZAP!! CRACKLE!!! POP!!** A tiny flume of smoke issues forth from the plastic strings of death. A smile forms on my lips. ***Gotcha, ya little bugger!*** Something about the killing racquet makes me feel vindicated for all the mosquito bites I've ever had. Meanwhile, Maizy disappeared. She doesn't feel the same about the racquet.

It had been a wet year. A good snow pack and spring rains lasting well into June all pointed to a bad mosquito summer. I knew I was going to have to take responsibility for my own happiness when hordes of mosquitoes descended on us all. There was no way the mosquito control board would be able to stave off what was to be a banner year. I was going to be super prepared. This wasn't my first mosquito rodeo.

I put new batteries in the racquet zappers, distributed cans of bug spray all over the house and yard, put screens on the doors, and strategized my new normal that would last until the first frost in either summer or fall. Citronella and Deet became my new perfume.

For several years during mosquito season, I would spend an inordinate amount of time slapping myself silly. My arms and legs got bruised and my poor face felt like it had been through a war. I wouldn't *think* when a mosquito landed on me, I *acted*. It was self-flagellation at its worst. I learned hesitation meant the mosquito escaped but for some reason, I slapped harder when I reacted quickly. I have knocked my glasses off more times than I can count. I've even given myself a fat lip or two. Boy, does that make me mad.

I've altered my tactics to rely on the racquet. It's so satisfying, and I've become pretty adept at improving and then maintaining my advancing age hand-eye coordination, not to mention the benefits of ambidextrous conditioning. Oh yeah, I can swing left or right-handed. When I go into the bathroom to brush my teeth at night, I start with a stalk of the walls and air, scanning and pouncing, as little toasted bodies float to the ground when the racquet of death finds each evil bug. I feel strong and powerful. I picture those little bubbles of words from the Batman show of my childhood appearing in the air near the kill sites, 'BAM! KAPOW! OOMPH! OW!' I brush my teeth smiling. It's a nice way to end the day.

The great outdoors is a whole different ballgame. The racquet is not nearly as effective out there so I am forced to use more drastic measures. I bring out the big guns, the large assortment of different kinds of sprays. There are so many choices. Some are natural and some are chemical. None of them are totally effective by themselves so the decision on what to use requires a deep knowledge of risk, tolerance, and longevity. Risk is about how toxic this stuff is and will I die too? Tolerance is about the mosquito population and energy levels of both the mosquitoes and me.

Longevity in the mosquito world is two-fold. If the mosquito is young, it is more stupid and spastic, thus making it more likely to die early in its life. Should it survive a day or two, it gets more desperate and annoying, and moves in like a Kamikaze pilot going after a destroyer. It strikes. I don't feel it until it punctures the skin, sending *'kill it'* receptors to my brain. Mosquito versus me. One of us always loses, often the mosquito.

I'm always open to learning new things. Especially when it comes to living in a mosquito ridden world. One year, in a supreme effort to mitigate having to use any kind of mosquito repellent with nasty chemicals like DEET, I decided to make up a batch of something I ran across on the internet purporting to control these nasty bloodsucking bugs.

In a big spray container went 3 cans of stale beer (I got the cheapest I could buy), a cup of Epsom salts, and a giant bottle of blue mouthwash. I'm still scratching my head about why it had to be blue but went with it although I may try other colors someday just to see if there is a difference. I walked all over the lawn, spraying away while trying to figure out the smell of it. Beer and mouthwash. It seemed familiar. Ah yes, I may have recognized it from my high school party girl days. Not some of my better judgement moments but oh well.

The good news is that it worked. The bad news is that when my sprinklers came on, it rapidly lost its effectiveness. Luckily, I got hit by something I like to call *'the lightning bolt of brilliance'* and adjusted my focus. Instead of the lawn, I spray it on my shrubs where mosquitoes love to hang out. Not only do the mosquitoes go away but my raspberries, elderberries, and sand cherries taste more delicious and my mouth is minty fresh. YAY!

Unfortunately, this concoction is not for spraying on my body, so I am stuck with the commercial chemical sprays. I have a long history with them.

I remember going out on a wildfire sometime in the early 1980s as part of a hand crew to build fire line. We were given bug repellent as part of our pack supplies. I only used it once. When I discovered it took the yellow paint off my pencil, I decided it probably wasn't good for my skin. I think it was Army surplus stuff from the Korean or Vietnam wars. It smelled horrible. If I was a mosquito, I wouldn't get anywhere near this stuff. It might have eaten a hole or two through my tee shirt. What the heck was in it?

Several years ago, there was a commercial on TV about *OFF!* mosquito spray. All it showed was a man's hairy arm with hundreds of mosquitoes on it. Then, his arm got sprayed with the *OFF!* and the mosquitoes jumped off his arm only to land again but this time, they weren't biting. Supposedly. It made me wonder why they called it *OFF!* when clearly the mosquiteos weren't exactly off. *They light but they don't bite!* At least, that's how I remember it. Whatever, I'm not buying it. It made me have nightmares of my body covered with mosquitos who lighted and weren't biting. It was creepy.

Nope, I use Cutter's. Why? Because it works and most importantly, I like the design on the can better. The colors speak to me and there's no picture of a mosquito anywhere in sight. I know all too well what a mosquito looks like. I don't need a giant picture on a can to tell me. Besides, Cutter's doesn't smell like a toxic insecticide, or so I tell myself.

However, if the mosquitoes are bad enough, I'll use anything. I'd even roll in mud. It might be fun.

Mosquito sprays have improved dramatically over the decades. I can now decide how much DEET I want, if any, and the odor is not unpleasant although if you inhale it while spraying, you will cough your brains out. I have tried many brands and chemical concoctions. I have great hope with each and every one. Citronella sprays are not toxic but they do have a lingering not very citrous like odor. Boy, does it linger. I'm pretty sure it must be oil based because it coats my nose hairs and they are hard to clean. It seems like everything has a downside. Then again, so do mosquito bites.

In my many conversations with God, I have yet to get any kind of good answer to the question of what He was thinking when He created mosquitoes, horseflies, and any other biting insects? I know it's not about the food chain because there are lots of other non-biting bugs that taste good and provide nourishment to the many things that eat them. I have wracked my brain trying to find ONE good reason mosquitoes exist. Nothing. Not even an inkling. Someday He and I will chat about this in person.

In the meantime, I know mosquitos suck in more ways than one. Now I just I need a rallying cry. I kind of like a very forceful and loud *'DIE SUCKER!'* Oh, and **KAPOW** and **BAM**!!! Maybe I'll come up with a happy dance as I watch little wisps of smoke come from a successful zap of the racquet. Yeah. Good times. Is it possible I may look forward to mosquito season, just a little bit?

~ 13 ~

AGING IS NOT FOR WIMPS

Coming to terms with the aging process is fraught with emotions that run the gamut from frustration to depression to anger to hopelessness. And if that isn't enough to kick your butt, one look in the mirror will nail down the fact that the sun has turned your tanned face into a canyon land of wrinkles.

Now that I have your attention, I want to explain the good news and it's pretty simple. **You. Are. Alive.** And you have a lot of choices to make about how to face the inevitable. Will you be a whining wimp or will you embrace the life you have left?

Guess what I'm doing!

About the time I turned 60, I realized my television could be heard outside, way far outside. Further astute observations led to noticing the radio in my truck was also pretty loud. My daughter was getting a bit frustrated with our in-person conversations by having to repeat herself constantly. I can always tell by the look on her face when her patience level is about to end. She does have a soft voice, I told myself. She needs to speak up, I told her. I had heard this very same thing from my dad for years. It is always the speaker's fault. Always.

Anyway, I'm too young to have hearing aids.

But, one day while I was wandering around Costco and passing the hearing center, I made a split-second decision. I took a deep breath and made an appointment to get tested. As the day approached for the testing, I contemplated cancelling or running away and pretending I was not really that bad. I'm too young. I can't afford this. I don't wanna. It was wimp speak to the max.

I got there, had a lovely chat with the technician, listened to his instructions, and commenced to follow them. Unlike other kinds of medical issues, and this one is, it was completely painless, at least physically. As I sat there, listening to different sounds and reacting, the truth of my situation became clear. When it was over, I looked over at my new friend and he smiled. He then showed me the results on a computer screen and explained, in terms I could follow AND hear, that my hearing wasn't that bad but there were certain tones where the hearing loss was over 50%. I pointed to the screen and said that really bad one must be the tone in my daughter's voice. I asked him how they had gotten ahold of it. We chuckled but I was serious.

While we talked about our daughters for a few minutes, he connected a set of hearing aids to the computer, typed a few keys, and voila! He unhooked the hearing aids and showed me how to put them in and how to adjust them. Then he said I should go walk around the store and hear what I've been missing.

It was AMAZING! Not only was the world louder, but it was also clearer. I hadn't realized how fuzzy or muffled my hearing had been until that moment. I heard the little sparrows up in the rafters of the store. I heard the ball bearings move in the wheels of my cart. I heard a fascinating discussion between a couple trying to decide which mix of bagels to buy. And then I heard a guy doing a demonstration for the Traeger smokers three aisles away. I made my way over and asked questions while listening to the pellets move through the auger and drop into the burn bowl. Plink, plink, plink. Next thing I knew, I was wheeling my way back to the hearing aid center with a new smoker. It turned out to be an expensive day.

Every time I go into my doctor for my annual checkup, I wonder what new age-related torture test will be necessary. Somewhere in my 40s I was forced against my will to get mammograms. Not every year but as I've aged, it has become an annual event I try to face bravely, but in my head, I'm thinking ouch, ouch, ouch. Mammograms are just evil and I hate them. On the other hand, the bone density test is a piece of cake. The most painful part of it may be getting on or off the table.

When I reached the age of 50, I knew deep in my soul I would be facing a new procedure, the dreaded colonoscopy. Nothing about it sounded good. Not the 'why we need to get them' and certainly not the actual procedure.

Sure enough, my doctor ended our appointment by setting me up for my first one. In her mind, and now mine, it was not optional. The surgical center called the next day and gave me a pep talk, like they could make me feel better about it. Actually, it was mostly informational about the date and time, when to start the cleansing process, what I could do and what I absolutely couldn't. Like eat. Anything. Within 12 hours of the appointment. They followed it all up with a thick package of instructions in the mail. The more I read, the more worried I got.

I picked up the cleansing kit from the pharmacy and continued my journey of worry. The day before I needed to go in, I read the instructions for the millionth time, proceeded to take some innocuous looking pills and drink the gallon of solution intended to clean out my entire digestive system. Suffice to say, it did, and quickly. The absolute worst part of the procedure, including the actual colonoscopy, was choking down the whole gallon of some of the nastiest tasting stuff ever. Actually, the taste was only slightly better than the consistency (think mucus). Bleck.

I made it to the center the next day with more than a little trepidation. I really had no idea what to expect and when I was led to a cold and kind of dark room and laid down on the table, they put this big warm heavy blanket on top of me. The doctor came in and introduced himself and gave me a short explanation of what to expect. I remember none of it, not then and not now. The nurse must have started the anesthesia because the next thing I knew I was looking at a computer screen showing a camera image of my colon. I remember thinking it was very pink and shiny, kind of pretty.

Somehow, I had awakened in the middle of the procedure and was watching the doctor and the camera inside my colon. When I spoke and told him I thought it was pretty, he looked over at me and said, *'you're awake'* like it was the most normal thing ever. He was stitching up a little place in my colon where he had removed a polyp. He then injected some black dye into the spot. And that's all I remember.

I was wheeled into recovery and parked for I don't know how long but when the doctor came in to tell me about what he had found, I think I knew what he was saying through the fog of my brain. Basically, there was only the one spot he felt he needed to remove and have biopsied. He had tattooed it so he could check it again in one year.

My first thought was, ONE YEAR? I thought this was a 10-year thing. But he explained he wanted to make sure whatever it was, didn't come back. My second thought was, I HAVE A TATTOO! My first and only to this very day. Wait until I tell my daughter who has several real tattoos. She'll be so proud. Until I tell her where it is.

Long story short, the polyp was benign. The next year, the tattoo site showed no sign of the polyp, and best of all, the cleansing solution was different than the first one which made whole experience much better. I was more worried about the solution than the polyp. Go figure.

Colonoscopies are not so bad after all. In fact, I'd rather have one of them than a mammogram. Way less painful. Think about it, you get to lie down with a warm blanket and wake up knowing you get to go eat. And you have no recollection of what happened in between. But don't think about it. Just do it. It may save your life.

Annual visits to the dermatologist have become part of my aging norm. Every year I go get a full body check with the goal of not having anything frozen or cut off. In the almost 15 years I've been going, I've only met that goal once. Sun damage from years of adolescent tanning and a career of working in the great outdoors have led to various forms of dermatological torture. Age spots, moles, and other weird bumps on my skin have appeared in a variety of shapes and sizes all over my arms, hands and face. I walk out with a few frozen spots that burn like crazy. They itch as they heal and then whatever was under each spot is magically gone.

It has taken a lot of self-restraint not to play connect the dots from time to time with whatever skin anomalies are left. I just want to see if I have any constellations to match those in the sky.

This year, when my dermatologist walked into the room with her little bottle of freezing stuff tucked under her arm, I told her she wasn't going to find anything because she'd already frozen about a million spots on my body over the years. She smiled and started her examination. I was holding my breath as she assessed the possibilities. When she pulled the bottle out from under her arm, I knew I was doomed. One on the side of my face and one on my forearm. Rats.

As she examined my scalp, I mentioned a spot that had been scabby for a few months. She looked it over and decided to biopsy it. Getting a lidocaine shot in the top of my head was way worse than the freezing thing. Off to the lab went a piece of my head and I waited to hear if it was benign. Unfortunately, it wasn't and I had to go back to have the whole thing cut out. It was a basal cell carcinoma. Despite another shot of lidocaine, I felt like she was augering into my brain. It didn't hurt, it just felt deep. She put two stitches inside the gaping hole and five more on the top of the hole.

The results came back from the lab saying she had gotten all the carcinoma. Whew. In the meantime, the hair was starting to grow back and I was left with a divot. Since I am a golfer, it's easy to visualize one of the many divots I've left on the courses. It just seems weird that this one is on the top of my head.

As I navigate through life and the everyday aches and pains, I continually amp up the pep talks. Wear sunscreen, eat more fiber, get off the couch, stay active, and engage with people every day.

What I do know is things aren't going to get any easier so I'm going to adapt to aging with as much grace and humor as I can. When I go in for my next annual physical, I'll try not to yell '*WHAT NOW?*' even though I'll want to. Instead, I will endure all the tests my doctor says I need with a smile and hope for no unpleasant surprises.

Who knows, maybe I'll end up with something as fun as a tattoo or a divot. Anyone want to see the pictures of my tattoo inside my colon? Come on, don't be a wimp.

~ 14 ~

WHAT ARE THE ODDS?

I like to think of myself as a trained observer of things most people don't give a second thought to. Little things that turn into big annoying things. These are things that may or may not make you question your sanity. Check this out:

It's been said that over time, the odds for pretty much anything are 50:50. So why is it when I pick up the cord to plug my phone in, I almost always have to turn it over to make it fit into the plug? At first, I thought I was imagining it so I started to really pay attention. I'm retired so it's no problem to focus on really important things like this.

Once I started paying attention, I realized it wasn't just my phone cord. Electrical wall sockets have a fat slot and a not fat slot. No matter how I approach the socket to plug something in, I almost always have to turn it over. I know what you are thinking. A smart person would look at the plug and the socket and have this figured out ahead of time to ensure a successful first-time outcome. I call that cheating. Besides, who has time for details like that? Oh right, smart people.

Another thing I almost always get wrong is USB plugins. Whether it's my computer, the printer, or the one in my truck, I am forced to emit a heavy sigh when I first try to plug it in. Should a miracle happen and I get it right on my first try, I almost have to fight back tears of joy.

The concept of 50:50 is not relevant in my life.

I decided to ask other people to see if it's just me or what. Because I tend to just jump right into something without providing anyone with any background information, I get a lot of blank stares when I casually ask someone if they have trouble plugging in their phones on the first try. If they happen to be like me, and rarely get it right on the first try, a look of understanding flashes over their faces that can only mean *'I'm not the only one! Whew!'*. We laugh and share stories of our awkward kinship of ineptitude. We are now comrades for life!

Okay, I may be exaggerating a wee bit but I'm still thinking of starting a support group.

Knowing the odds are more like 80:20 against me, gambling is something I've sort of learned to avoid. Oh, I've tried it and guess what, I might as well just throw my money in the garbage. I've tried all kinds of strategies to prove myself wrong. I pretend not to care as I throw five dollars into a slot machine one quarter at a time and two minutes later, it's all gone. Where's the fun in that? I know, I know, slot machines have the worst odds but what if my horrible record could work for me? Just once.

I've actually done weird things to trick a machine to not know it's me. I sneak up like I'm not going to play and then throw in a quarter, pull the handle really fast, and step away. Another twenty-five cents down the drain. I watch other losers walk away from a machine and think, okay, my turn, this next pull will be a winner and guess what. Well, I didn't need that quarter anyway.

And cards? Yet another lesson in humility. If it's a game with a partner, I become that poor kid who gets picked last on the team. I immediately start apologizing to whoever drew the short stick and got me as their partner. The good news is I don't play any card game for real money. I play because it's fun and it generates a lot of laughter and comradery, sometimes even deep, meaningful discussions. Who cares about winning? I've certainly learned not to.

I almost lost my best friend because of gin rummy.

She and I worked for several months in the great outdoors in the middle of nowhere Wyoming. Since there was no television, we'd end our days by playing gin rummy. The mistake we made was keeping score. She kicked my butt night after night. I could have shuffled the cards for an hour and she would still draw a better hand. I'd get what I thought was a winning hand only to go down within seconds because hers was better. If I had known how to cheat, she still would have won.

Every time she started to put her cards down, I would yell *'NO!!!!'* and I would sit there holding all my cards, knowing my minus score was going to get worse. We played to 500 points and she'd get there while I was sitting at almost -500. It was humiliating. I'd pout. I'd stalk away. I'd say mean things. And yet, we continued to play. I don't know why.

It makes my stomach hurt just remembering it. When it comes to gin rummy, the odds are more like 99:1 against me. How is this possible? Had we played for money, like a penny a point, I'd prob-ably owe her over a million dollars....

We are still friends, good friends. She thinks it's funny I was such a drama queen. I was not. She thinks I exaggerate. I do not. We have not played gin rummy since that summer. I value our friendship too much.

I have gotten smarter over time. Instead of actually playing, I was a BINGO caller at the local nursing home. I'm pretty good at it. I learned to turn the crank on the BINGO ball holder cage just right so the balls fall down into the holder thingy. If I turn it too fast, nothing comes out. Too slow and the balls don't even get to the holder thingy. When I picked up a ball and called out O75, I used a lovely sing song voice and then ran around to make sure everyone put a mark on their cards if they had it. Then I raced back to the ball rack and to call out another number.

Sometimes, I got to have a partner so I didn't have to run around as much but I did have to keep an eye on things. BINGO is a serious game for most of these players and they don't appreciate it if my partner and I don't keep things moving along. I didn't have to worry about beating the odds but I did have to act like I didn't care who won. Sometimes I'd find myself cheering for who I thought were the underdog. In my very own made-up test, I discovered I was sealing their BINGO fate by playing favorites. I had the curse for the difference between winning and losing. I apologized often.

This holds true for sports teams I like. There is a reason the Min-nesota Vikings have never won a Superbowl. They are my team. If I watch them play, they lose. If I don't watch, they win. They should pay me not to watch. Maybe, if I don't watch any of their games all season, they'll actually get to a Superbowl and then I'll have to go somewhere where there's no chance I'll see any of it. Their odds of winning would immediately go up. Yup, they should pay me. I wonder who I can contact about it.

So, now that you know all this, is there something wrong with me? And don't say *'Yeah, you're a Vikings fan'* or you will no longer be my friend. My proven inability to beat the odds at pretty much any-thing, is just another oddity in the wonderful world of being alive. I've learned to adapt and accept it. Sometimes, as with so much else in life, it's all I can do.

THE PERFECT DOG SHOW

One Thanksgiving a few years ago, I found Little Mother watching a rerun of an American Kennel Club dog show after having finished eating and experiencing the usual post-meal lethargy. She was channel surfing and had settled on the National Dog Show. I sat down to watch with her.

These dogs are the best of the best of their breed. They seem to be well behaved and get lots of treats while some stranger checks their teeth, legs and rear ends. Then they prance around the ring and stand in a line with the rest of the dogs until someone is declared the winner. There are no dog fights, butt sniffing, barking or other inappropriate behavior. Thinking about my dogs, I had to wonder, how is this possible?

I have two puppies. Maizy is a 14-month-old Pembroke Welsh Corgi and Tank is an 8-month-old half Cardigan Corgi and half Australian Shepherd. Both are driving me crazy. They have so much energy they make me tired. What was I thinking when I got two dogs that are puppies at the same time? Oh right, they are beyond cute and I love them!

In the time that I've had them, we have worked on basic commands like 'sit' and 'down' and 'STOP BARKING' to varying degrees of success. What I've come to believe is I need more training than they do. I am not ashamed to admit it.

I have the perfect setup at my house to let them romp and play inside and outside. There is a nice big fenced yard and a dog door so that they can go in and out whenever they want to. We also go for walks out in the great outdoors and everyone gets tired. We walk for miles, untethered and free until we are literally and figuratively pooped out. Yes, we are lucky and somewhat spoiled.

Any time we take a trip to somewhere outside our carefree home front, things are a bit different. It becomes all too real when I come face to face with having to put them on leashes to go anywhere. To add to the experience, I get to carry little bags to pick up their poop because they **always** poop on a walk. Then I get to carry it around until I can dispose of it properly. None of us like this change in our situation. There is nothing quite like picking up warm poop first thing in the morning, gifts from two excited puppies on leashes.

Tank chews through leashes like a ninja. I never see it happen. After cobbling the same leash back together several times in one short walk, I realize I have a lot of work to do. While carrying my little bags of warm dog poop and untangling the two leashes from the directionally challenged pair of puppies for the umpteenth time, I decided to get on board with some serious training. It was either that or make a call to see if there were any openings at the local psych ward.

As the dog show droned on and on, I decided to take my little furry friends for a walk. While watching them sniff every single thing along the way, my mind began to wander. What if there was a dog show for untrained people with untrained puppies? It would be a gross understatement to say it would be way different than the genteel, controlled, well dressed, groomed to the gnat's eyebrow, affair.

The rules would be simple:
Rule 1- all dogs would have to be less than two years old.

Rule 2- instead of dog breeds, the categories would be about the size of the puppy. The categories would be Tiny, Little, Medium, Medium Large, Large, Extra Large and Super Big. Each dog would be sized by boxes that the owners would place them in to see what category they fit into. This might be the most entertaining way to start a competition ever imagined. I haven't met a puppy yet that wanted to be put into a box without it turning into some kind of game.

And oh yeah, Rule 3-all the puppies have to be mixed breeds. No purebreds allowed.

Rule 4- The puppy and the owner compete together. There would be no non-owner handlers. No one gets to have someone else do their dirty work or have all the fun.

Rule 5- is a bit more complicated. The owner would use a 10-foot retractable leash with no brakes. In other words, the owner has to let the puppy go as far as the leash will allow. It can retract but it can't be stopped or held shorter than 10 feet unless the puppy choses to be closer to its owner. Still, this would probably promote the maximum possible uncontrolled glee for the puppy. There's no telling how the owner will feel about it besides panicked.

Rule 6- Treats and poop bags are mandatory items that the owner must have at all times. Each time the puppy does something really adorable, it gets a treat. Should the puppy need to eliminate his or her stomach contents from either of his or her end, the owner has 5 seconds to scoop or clean up the stuff without gagging or they will be eliminated from the competition and sent nearby until the closing ceremony. If successful, the owner then has 10 seconds to get to the nearest waste receptacle and dispose of it with a flourish. Flourishes have point value. Owner barfing is not a flourish. Don't worry, waste receptacles would be placed everywhere.

There are only two events and they are designed to give everyone a chance to shine.

The first event is where each puppy and owner team make one lap around the arena together. Neither can be dragged. This is a timed event and comprises only part of the point total. Should dragging occur, the team will stop until both puppy and owner have composed themselves. There is no limit on how many times this can happen but because it is a timed event, it's best if no dragging occurs. Treats can be consumed by either team member. Alcohol is not a treat.

At the end of the lap, each owner and dog team get to sit down to compose themselves and rest until every team is done. Once this event is done, the next one starts.

The second and final event is what everyone comes for, audience and participants alike. It is the event where everyone without a dog, and not related to either dog or owner, gets to be a judge. Every audience member gets a whiteboard and a dry erase pen.

Each team has 5 minutes to get dressed up. Owner and dog must change into adorable matching outfits. Points are awarded for creativity, ability to keep all dress up items on for a full minute, and how well they match each other. One at a time, a puppy and owner step forward. A couple big screen TVs show an up close and personal look at them. The audience judges quickly hold up their scoring for each team. A team of tally masters makes notes of the scores.

Scoring is as follows: 1-nice try, thank you for coming; 2-you two are a great pair but you could do better; 3-the puppy is cute but you need to step it up; 4-you are so close but 80s clothing went out a long time ago for good reason; and 5-TWINS! YOU LOOK LIKE TWINS! GOOD JOB!

Finally, all dogs and owners get to take a break while the tally masters add up all the scores. There are tally masters for each size category because everyone needs a fun job. When the scores for both events come in the owners and puppies are directed to spread out in a large circle by size. The anticipation builds. A carefully chosen announcer with a great announcing voice, enters and stands in the middle of the circle dressed like a dog biscuit wearing a hard hat. He or she thank all who came, all who participated with their dogs, and all the sponsors. It's only polite to be grateful.

The announcer tells everyone to get ready to find out the winners and scurries out of the circle while yelling **'You all are!!!'** This is the prearranged signal and the next thing we see is a big net lowered from the ceiling. As it is released just above the circle, dog treats and toys of all sizes and kinds begin to hit the ground. Everyone gets busy filling pockets and bags with dog booty. Dogs are running around with toys or treats in their mouths, all smiling. It's a dream come true for every dog here because in this dog show everyone is a winner. The end.

Speaking of dreams, Tank and Maizy have managed to wrap themselves around my legs again, and as I start to fall, my perfect dog show reverie is broken. The two bags of warm dog poop fly from my hands as I try to catch myself. Fortunately, there were no injuries to dogs or me but I'm not sure I'm going to give those two little dogs a treat. Who am I kidding?

As I stumble into the house with my two little balls of furry happiness, Little Mother calls out, *'How was your walk?'* I thought about explaining my great idea about the perfect dog show but I think you'd have to be there. In my head. At best, a questionable place to be.

Instead, I asked her if I should put the poop bags in the recycle or regular garbage cans.

~ 16 ~

A CUT ABOVE....OR TO THE SIDE

Feel the excitement!! Time for a teaching moment.
This is the base of a roadcut. Feel smarter?
Oh, I have more to share! Read on.

When I retired, one of the first things I did was travel. The wonder of retirement and traveling allowed my brain to slow down since I wasn't in a hurry anymore. I was finally able to observe lots of new things I had not taken the time to see because my mind was on other things like work and life when not at work. You know, life in high gear.

One day I was driving from Helena, Montana heading north to Shelby, Montana to pick up a friend coming in on the train. I had driven this route many times over the years but hadn't ever really paid attention to anything but driving. Interstate 15 cuts through Wolf Creek canyon which later follows along the Dearborn and Missouri rivers. The rock formations were spectacular but what really caught my eye were the roadcuts. I didn't get to spend much time studying them while going 70+ miles an hour but the seed was planted. I wanted to learn more.

For those of you who don't know what a roadcut is, it's a place where the road was cut *through* a hill or mountain rather than building the road *over* the hill or mountain. They are everywhere, especially in the west. I decided to make it my mission to open the eyes of the world to the wonders of roadcuts.

Roads take us from where we are to where we want to be. Unless there is something wrong with them, like potholes or construction, we pretty much take them for granted. As we drive, we tend to focus on innocuous things like safety *(staying in our own lane)* and the endless thoughts in our minds dealing with everyday life *(what am I going to make for dinner?)*. What we don't do is look around. We are so busy chasing our tails, we don't notice what is right in front, and a little to the sides of us as we blaze through glorious landscapes and roadcuts.

I managed to take a lot of pictures of roadcuts over the next several months. Really pretty ones and really boring ones. I was going to write an entire book about roadcuts. I was going to explain, in great detail, what each roadcut was all about. The geological story without it being a drain on anyone's brain, including mine. The book was going to be epic and super interesting. Everyone who read it would see roads in a whole new way and thank me for opening up this whole new world.

When I found out how much it costs to print a book in color, I hung my head and pouted for few days. I knew black and white pictures would never do justice to the beauty of roadcuts.

You might wonder what ever possessed me to come up with this concept. Sometimes, I wonder what possesses my brain too. I'm not worried. Yet.

After about a year into retirement I realized I needed a purpose. Life had finally slowed down a bit. I was now travelling for fun. Long trips, short trips, some on foot, some using conveyances like cars, planes, and trains. I started noticing my surroundings instead of just the endpoint. Lo and behold, there are **a lot** of interesting things going on all around us and what's more, most aren't even moving. We are, but they aren't.

So, what did I do? (*I know you are hanging on the edge of your seat. Admit it.*) I stopped. (*Was that too anticlimactic?*) Sometimes I stopped to let the dogs out to use the 'facilities' and would just let my gaze slowly take in all 360 degrees of where we were. It takes a lot of practice to gaze slowly. It requires a lot of focused self-talk and mindful breathing techniques I acquired when I had tried to learn how to meditate. I never really caught on to meditation but taking a moment to just look at something new was just relaxing. And fascinating. That's how I discovered roadcuts and other subtleties of the world around us.

I will admit stopping for roadcuts is a bit problematic, especially when pulling a camper. I learned to scout for possibilities when I saw a roadcut with potential coming up. I would slow, put on my blinker, and start easing over to the side of the road. If it looked promising, I would stop and put my warning lights on. If it looked boring, I'd punch the gas, put my other blinker on and continue on my merry way. Sometimes I'd get flipped off but having owned a 1969 Volkswagen camper bus years ago, I was used to it and didn't take it personally. Volkswagen buses weren't known for their speed or ability to accelerate but luckily road rage was limited to the middle finger wave as we were constantly passed on any or every roadway. Too bad I wasn't into roadcuts back then. I could have taken pictures while we were moving.

Now whenever I stop, I grab my camera and take a few shots. I think about what drew me to this particular roadcut. Why is it not boring? What created it? My limited geology-terminology brain is throwing out words like igneous, sedimentary, and folds and up-lifts, synclines and anticlines.

All the blood that had been pooled in my rear end from driving is redistributed and I feel a need to take a closer look.

As I walk along the base of a roadcut, the intricacies of rocks *in situ* become more apparent and the story of millions and billions of years is speaking to me. Okay, that may be a bit dramatic but there is some truth to it. The roadcut does tell a story. It may be about a volcanic event or a lake covering half of North America, or glaciers forming and then melting. It's alive even though it's rock. How does that work?

Every once and a while I have a willing victim in the truck with me. A few springs ago I took Little Mother on a drive. We both needed to get outside after a long winter and it seemed like a good way to spend some quality time. We drove north from Helena, Montana, towards Great Falls through Wolf Creek Canyon. It's a winding road through part of the Big Belts Mountain range so there are a LOT of roadcuts. We eventually moved off the freeway onto the frontage road so we didn't feel rushed. Little Mother didn't know she was going to be part of my *'Are roadcuts interesting?'* focus group.

About halfway through the canyon, I stopped and pointed out a roadcut with all kinds of interesting layers and colors. In my teaching voice I talked about how this area had once been a lake for a really long time and this was all sedimentary formation millions of years old. We looked at some of the folding rock layers going on in parts of it and had quite the conversation about it all and sounded really smart.

About ten miles up the canyon, we ran into another formation, totally different. Luckily, there was a rest stop where she needed to use the facilities. I didn't have that need so I wandered over and read the interpretive signs about a volcano that happened in the area 75,000 years ago. I was able to wow her with all kinds of facts using my happy voice. Teaching moments go much better with a happy voice. My Little Mother is a bit of a rockhound too so she was an enthusiastic supporter in the focus group. And we created a great mother/daughter memory. Yay!

I've been managing to convert just about everyone who has had the pleasure of my company on a drive. I drive just fast enough that no one can jump out while I explain the beauty and nature of roadcuts. If I don't know what we're seeing, I make stuff up using all kinds of geological terms I've read about. Later, I do a little research to see if I was anywhere close to being right. Sometimes I am. Other times, it's just a good story.

I probably have hundreds of roadcut pictures from all over the west. I can't seem to stop taking pictures of them. The features stir my imagination and fire my aging synapses. If I ever get rich, I will write that dang roadcut book. Not only are they fascinating, they bring back great memories of my travels and adventures.

Speaking of adventures, anyone game to go on one? I promise it won't be boring. Just take everything I say with a grain of salt. Or sand.

~ 17 ~

HAPPY HAIR DAYS

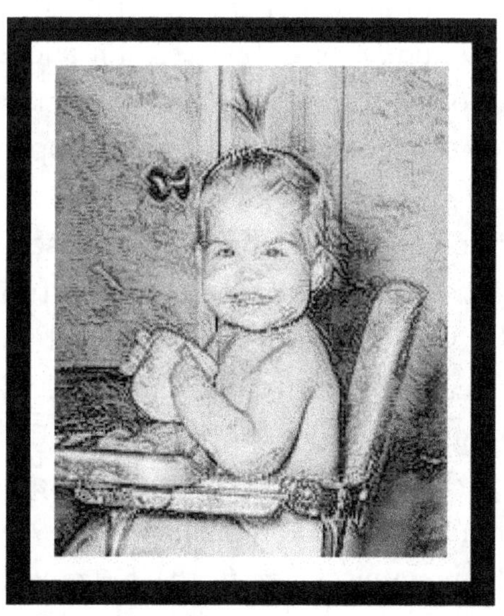

From this lovely hairdo to.....

As I look back on my life, one of the things I periodically reflect on are my various hair styles. I'll be sitting in my den where I either read or write and find myself staring vacantly at the wall of family pictures. As I wake myself up and try to refocus, I see the history of my family going back to the 1800s. I realize hairstyles are either really adorable or really awful no matter what generation and there is a photographic record of it. Eeek!

Probably my most favorite hair style was from a time I don't remember. I think I was about one year old and I'm pretty sure all moms who have had girls, loved the simplicity of one particular style. I don't know the technical name but I call it 'the palm tree'. Mom would gather up all my hair and bring it to the top of my head, put a rubber band around the base of it and let go. What little hair I had, spread out like, well, a palm tree. In every picture I've seen from those days, I look spectacular. And super happy.

Later, my sisters and I had hair styles also designed by our mother. She was the queen of creating the straightest bangs in the history of the world. We all had identical bangs. I think the style was a holdover from mom's days in college. I know this to be true from watching old movies on the Turner Classic channel. All the women had perfect bangs. If I had had the ability to articulate my misgivings about straight and perfect bangs, I would have said, *'Mom! Get with the program. We're in the 1960s now, not the 1940s!'* I wouldn't have been able to sit down for a few days but I would have made my feelings known.

Every Easter Sunday for about four years during our elementary school days, our mom would dress us up in new hats, dresses she'd sewn, and shiny patent leather shoes. Brother Bruce got a buzz haircut, a shirt that was buttoned up to the neck, and pants with perfect creases down the legs.

In addition, we girls got our mom's version of a home beauty salon. She'd sit us down and proceed to tie our hair up in rags. Yes, rags. They were soaked in water and then rolled up in our hair like curlers. Then, she'd put us to bed and in the morning, take out the rags. We had curls out the ying-yang. After a short period of styling and dressing, we were marched to a place where she would take our pictures. We always felt so pretty. I don't remember where we went from there to display our cuteness. Sunday school at church or maybe Easter buffet at the Officer's Club, just some kind of outing to make it worth all the trouble she went to.

For the longest time, age 6 to 13, all I remember about my hair was growing it out. I went from having a short bob with bangs to no bangs and no real style. It was straight as a board and took forever to get any length to it. But, every school picture from first grade through junior high was more about my teeth than my hair. When my baby teeth came out in first grade, they were replaced by gigantic permanent teeth. I could have been bald and no one would have noticed because my huge buck teeth defined my entire head.

The only thing added to my hair 'style' was stretchy headbands to keep the hair out of my face. I had every color of headband there was but the price for being able to see without my hair covering my face was the feeling that my ears were sticking out unnaturally because the headbands were tucked behind them. I like to call this my ugly duckling stage of life.

By the time I got to high school, I had lived through braces and dropped the headbands. It was the early 1970s and everyone had long, straight hair, parted in the middle. Even the boys. The exception was my brother who got a haircut from dad every week. He was not cool. His hair reflected poorly on my high school coolness.

I begged my dad to let my brother grow his out a bit but he was adamant about his only son not looking like a girl. With those haircuts, there was no mistaking gender.

Our long straight hairstyles didn't require a lot of work or creativity. If we got really wild, we'd take small strands from the front and tie them to the back of our heads. The style was wash it, brush it and go and it worked for years. All of my yearbook pictures can attest to it.

Along came the age of mullets and perms, the 1980s. I kind of feel like this deserves some kind of dirge music as a background to the concept of such travesties.

At some point in the early part of the decade, I felt the need for a change in my life so I got both, first the perm and then the mullet. I had long puffy hair with the sides trimmed up to the middle of my ears and flat bangs. I was hip. I was now. I am still finding pictures of myself to burn.

I thought I looked pretty dang good and I kept up that illusion by maintaining both the perm and the mullet for at least four years. I did add bangs back into my life towards the end of this period but they didn't quite make up for the number of times I sat in a chair and allowed my hair to be permed and burned.

I finally got out of this rut and cut my hair to about shoulder length so I could tolerate growing out the mullet layer. The time it takes to grow the sides to match the length of the rest of my hair is interminable. Months of aggravation finally paid off and the mullet days became just an unpleasant memory.

I kept up with the perms at this length for many years until one day I went to my haircutter person and told her I was tired of my hair and needed to do something bold. I ended up with the most comfortable hairstyle ever. We chopped it all off. Sort of. It was short with some layering and boy did I feel good. Light as a feather. I've kept it at a short to mid-short length ever since. It's a style that keeps on giving.

First off, it doesn't get all tangled so there is no pain when I brush it out. Second, it takes no time to dry after washing. I just brush it out and go. If I get really wild, I might use a hairdryer to give it a little punch. Third, and the best part of all, is the myriad of bedhead looks that greet me in the mirror every morning. It's very important to start the day with a laugh.

I do this by dragging myself out of bed and looking in the mirror to see how I've survived the night. I pop around the corner in the bathroom to the mirror like a sideways jack-in-box. I'll be honest and mention that I don't consciously work hard on my hair in case you haven't figured it out by now. Unlike most women who use hair products, curling irons, brushes or combs and blow dryers, my most amazing hairdo comes from using a CPAP mask (for sleep apnea), a pillow, and having a nightly wrestling match with two dogs and two cats for control of the bed.

Just when I think it can't get any better, I will surprise myself with a look that appears like I've stuck my finger in a light socket. Sometimes, I'll take a selfie just so I can look at it throughout the day and laugh.

As I age, I am watching my hair turn gray. It's fascinating. There are sections where there is more gray than dark brown and I wonder about how the hairs know when to change and then, why in groups of gray? Will it ever be totally gray or will it eventually turn white like my mom's? I guess I'll find out.

Maybe I'll end up with hair more like my dad's. He managed to keep some dark hair all the way into his 80s, especially in his moustache. I've been checking my moustache and so far, so good.

It'll be interesting to see where my hairstyles go from here. With age comes wisdom so I know what I will never do to it again. I recently went to a new hair stylist and tried to explain what I wanted. The first words out of her mouth were, *'I will not give you a mullet.'* How did she know? Hmmm, maybe subconsciously I still want one.

I am so glad there are people out there willing and brave enough to talk me down from disaster.

...Crazy psychopath

~ 18 ~

THE HARD WAY

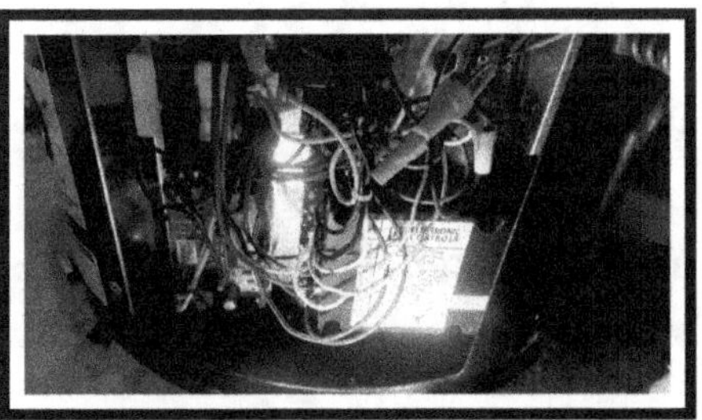

Are we surprised this didn't work?

Now doesn't this look better?

I really am a fairly competent person. Good grief, I've been alive long enough so I better be. Experience has taught me many things but it's baffling how many of those things I have to learn repeatedly. For instance, when it comes to plumbing anything, I always hold my breath after I've 'fixed' something.

A couple years ago the hot water heater in my house decided to call it quits. It had served the house well for many years and one day it just stopped working. Normally, this would not be such a big deal but this water heater not only provided the domestic hot water but also the radiant floor heating. The timing couldn't have been worse. It was January. In Montana.

I pulled out the paperwork for the water heater and made some calls. That particular brand was not available anywhere nearby. I thought since I knew it worked well with the house system needs, I should get the same thing. Sound reasoning? I thought so.

I got online and found the brand and model and ordered it. When it showed up, I was so happy. I had a plumbing and heating company come and install it. Finally, I had hot water.

A few months later, it quit. What? It's brand new. So, back came the plumber guys who called the company I bought it from and they managed to get it going. For the next two years, I ended up employing several different plumber-heating company people to work on keeping the dang thing running. They blamed the water heater company who blamed the installers. I just wanted it to work.

Every time it broke down, I channeled my pioneer spirit and heated water on the stove to do simple things like dishes or mopping floors. I used every friend I had to let me take a shower at their house. All my laundry was done using cold water and was thankful I didn't have to toil over a washboard and hang the clothes out to dry.

I think the whole experience gave me a little bit of PTSD because whenever I turned on the hot water faucet to take a shower, I would stand there hoping against hope for hot water, holding my breath. As soon as I let my guard down and felt like it was going to keep working, it would quit.

Finally, I had had enough. I totally replaced the relatively new unit with an on-demand system. Not only did it take up a lot less space, it hardly used any propane. The water turned hot after a short period of time and it kept the house as warm as I need it to be.

After thousands of dollars, showering in lots of different homes, huddling next to my back up heat source for days and days, and wondering why it always seemed to break down in the winter and never when it was warm outside, I think the whole nightmare is finally over. I don't hold my breath anymore when I turn on the hot water faucet, waiting for any sign of warmth, knowing it might not get warm. I don't sink to the depths of despair or yell at the heavens words to the effect of 'WHY ME?'. I don't wake up in the morning and see my breath because it's so bloody cold. I am whole again and life is good.

Still, I wonder. What was wrong with my thinking in the first place? Why do I feel like I have to learn every little thing the hard way? It's not just the whole hot water heater debacle.

I recently changed out the kitchen sink faucet. The old one was leaking again so I decided it was time to just start over. Sister Tracey *(who is not a nun)*, came up to visit and since she and I had replaced the one at her house years ago, we figured we had this down. We took out the old one, read through the instructions for the new one and proceeded to install it. It all went well until I decided to shorten the supply pipes because the new setup didn't need them to be so long.

Needless to say, I should have left well enough alone. Why does the little voice in my head tell me not to do this? It seems straightforward and reasonable. Apparently, I'm a terrible listener. I broke the supply pipe when I tried to shorten it and water shot everywhere. As I raced downstairs to shut off the main water line, I spent a few moments beating myself up. Again.

Every fall, I winterize my little Rpod trailer to keep the pipes from freezing and breaking. The first year I did this, I learned how important it was to unhook the waterline to the toilet. When I turned the water on in the spring, it shot all over the bathroom from a break on the toilet connection. About $25 later and having watched several YouTube videos on how to replace it, I patted myself on the back when I turned the pump back on and didn't see water shooting anywhere.

The next year spring comes along and I'm out camping. It's time to take a shower. I had already turned on the hot water heater and waited for it to get hot. Next, I got the towel moved to a handy place to use when I'm done and then I got undressed. I turned on the faucet in the shower and waited for the water to turn warm. It didn't. It was ice cold. So, I got dressed, went out and checked the hot water heater. It sounded like it was working. I reset the hot water switch and tried again. This time I didn't bother to get undressed. I just turned on the faucet again and it was still ice cold.

My brain was racing trying to figure out why the hot water tank is hot but the water wasn't. Aha! Did I check the valves under the bed when I de-winterized? Probably not. So, I lifted up the bed, took out the wood panel covering the pump and hot water heater and checked the valves. I had missed a valve. Whoops. How could that be? Yes, it is like a jungle of water lines under there. Once again, minor details derail my confidence. Dang it.

Finally, I could take a shower. And I do. As I'm drying off, I wonder why it is I have to learn things the hard way all the time. At least it feels like all the time.

The third year of trailer travails is also related to the shower. I had already replaced the shower head once because I hadn't drained it the previous year and it froze and broke, so water shot through the length of the handle instead of the head. Since that time, I've learned to drain the shower head as part of the winterizing process. This time, I had just hung the head from the attachment down the wall thinking it would drain and if there was anything left in the line, it would be RV antifreeze. The next spring, I was out in the middle of Utah camping with sister Tracey *(who is not a nun)*. We both needed a shower so I got the hot water heater going, got all ready for a nice shower and lo and behold, the shower head shot water out the handle but not the head. Again.

And then I remembered seeing a gallon jug of RV antifreeze in my garage that spring that not only froze solid but pushed the liquid up out of the jug and leaked all over the garage floor. Isn't antifreeze not supposed to freeze, thus the name?

It doesn't seem to matter if I do things right, the universe conspires to remind me it is my lot in life to learn things the hard way. I'm beginning to feel like it's the only way I'll ever learn anything.

Maybe it's telling me I made a brilliant career choice in not becoming a plumber. Fine. I get it.

In the meantime, I'm going to put a couple of extra showerheads in the trailer. Just in case.

~ 19 ~

FAMILY FEUD

Back in the good old days when there weren't any electronics, our family would sit down together for some old-fashioned fun every once in a while. One of the perks of having three siblings was being able to while away the days when the weather wasn't very cooperative by playing board games. It was either do that or do unfun things like clean our rooms. Television viewing was limited to Sunday evening or Saturday morning.

One of my favorite games was when Dad would get out a map of the world and challenge us to find countries he would randomly throw out. 'Find Japan.' 'Find Belgium.' We'd race our fingers all over the map to see who could find it first. Later, he'd ask what the capital of some country was and we'd find the country and look for the capital. Pronunciation of some of the capitals was not important but it could be entertaining. This parenting tool was pretty effective for teaching geography without your kids knowing they were learning something.

113

When the four of us got older, Dad got out the box of AAA state maps. He'd unfold one and tell us to find some town in the state on the map. He'd start with cities. Then it got harder. The cities turned to towns and then little bitty towns. We'd pour over it, trying to find them. First one to find it, won. We thought it was all about winning while getting to know a state. It wasn't. It was spending time with our dad.

When my two younger sisters weren't playing with dolls and Barbie, brother Bruce and I managed to cajole them into games like Chutes and Ladders and Candyland. It was always competitive and often ended with tears and at least one person angrily leaving the game. Later, we grew up. Sort of. Around the time I reached the ripe old age of about 12, maybe 13, we graduated to more challenging games like Life and Monopoly. Both required strategy and money management. Since I am the oldest, I clearly thought I had an advantage over my younger siblings. In retrospect, I was delusional at a young age.

The problem with these games is they last FOREVER. It wasn't tears that ended the playing because we rarely got to the point where a winner could be declared. But it kept us busy for hours and Mom was happy unless she had to break up a fight.

At some point in our lives, the game of Tripoley was introduced as a whole family kind of card game. It involved playing three different games using one deck of cards; Michigan rummy, Hearts, and Poker. We loved it because it was strategic, we got real poker chips, and Mom and Dad played. We felt like adults because of the poker chips. At some point during the playing, there would be a break and everyone would either run for the bathroom or make root beer floats for all of us. Now that I think about it, it was always the female contingent of the family making the floats. Hmmm.

Dad, being the family artist, had made a large Tripoley plastic tablecloth. He painted the suit symbols on the corners, added the parts for each of the games so we knew where to place our chips, and added little Dad touches to make it ours. Whenever it was time to play, one of us would have the honor of getting the poker chips, cards, and tablecloth out. Game on!!!

The most memorable game for me was the time when I won it all in one hand. During one of the breaks, while we girls were making the root beer floats, and Dad was in the bathroom, it was brother Bruce's turn to be the dealer. He was left alone at the table to shuffle and deal the cards. When we all got back to the table, he had each of the piles he had dealt sitting in front of him. One by one, he passed them all out to us. As I picked up my pile and proceeded to sort them in my hand, I noticed an amazing thing. The entire hand was all hearts. Not only that, there were all the high cards from the other suits. I was going to shoot the moon and leave everyone in the dust. For the first time ever in my life, I was speechless. I looked up and noticed Bruce staring at his hand like the most confused person ever. It was then I knew he was a cheater. He had stacked the deck while we were all out of the room and given me his cards by mistake.

I had a big decision to make, play or come clean. I'm not going to lie. It was all I could do to keep it together. If I had any semblance of a poker face, this was the time to use it. Again, since I am the oldest of the four of us kids, I decided it was time to teach my little brother a lesson. As we started the first of the three games, I managed to win every hand without exploding. I kept looking at his miserable face and slapping down winning cards with gusto.

All good things come to an end. I couldn't stop the tears from leaking out of my eyes while trying not to laugh. Finally, I laid down my entire hand on the table for all to see. All those hearts, all those high cards. If I could have kept going, I would have won every single game and declared 'TRIPOLEY!!!' I couldn't do it. All heads turned to Bruce, the dealer. And then we all started to laugh. He had spent the entire break time pulling all those cards and putting them in order. It was genius.

When we all graduated from high school and moved off to college, the summers and various holiday breaks would bring us back together again for more games. Trivial Pursuit was one we tried and one where we all finally admitted to the whole wide world that our parents were really smart. During the teenage angst years, we thought we knew everything. Now we were semi-adults and playing a game where we had to know something. We soon came to understand that lack of life experience and paying attention to nothing but ourselves was a disadvantage. College had yet to teach us about all the trivial details in the world around us. Later I would learn college didn't even come close to teaching us about many things to help win at Trivial Pursuit.

If we played in teams, we'd try to get one of our parents on our team. They seemed to know the answers to almost anything. Most of the time we played it without teams and there were categories we each excelled in or totally stunk in. I remember one time I had my pie almost filled in and I just needed to get that last piece. I think the category was 'DIFFICULT' and the name just psyched me out so I couldn't answer a single question right. Around and around the board I'd go, trying to land on the color I needed only to be stymied by the hardest question ever. Someone else would fill up their pie before I could so I never won.

We decided to try Pictionary. Sadly, only two people in our family can draw. I'm pretty good at stick figures but how the other non-artists would do was a mystery. We broke up into three teams. I wanted Dad to be my teammate because he was the real deal when it came to art. I couldn't even read brother Bruce's handwriting so I didn't want him. Sister Tracey did a lot of drafting and she could be a good partner. Sister Wendy and mom were questionable artists but Wendy was left-handed like me so that was her value. It doesn't make sense to me either. As it turned out, Mom was a better partner than Dad.

The one time I got to have Dad as a partner was a disaster. He got the clue, the timer was set, and I was ready. He proceeded to draw a courtroom. I called out words and he'd shake his head. He added the jury box with people, the witness stand, the defense and the prosecution tables with people, and finally the judge. On the judge's desk he drew the gavel and a tiny statue of the lady holding the scales of justice. Time had long since run out but he didn't want to quit until I got it. He pointed at the scales of justice repeatedly. I said things like 'statue', 'scales' or when he took his pen and circled the whole courtroom, I said 'courtroom'. He deflated, I hung my head, several members of my family had taken impromptu bathroom breaks, and finally he showed me the clue. My whole head filled with the words, *scales of justice* and it's never left.

When it was my turn to draw, I used the only art I knew, stick figures. In no time he figured out the clue but his words to me went something like *where did I go wrong?* Sometimes it's better to keep it simple.

I miss those days.

In looking back, I really couldn't tell you who won any of the games. Oh, it was competitive in the heat of battle but it was never about winning. Okay, maybe a little tiny bit. It was family time. The best kind of time in my life with my most favorite people in the world. Hard to beat that.

~ 20 ~

RESOLUTE RESOLUTIONS

The first day of the new year begins the season of making resolutions. A time for self-improvement. For many people, myself included, these usually revolve around weight loss, being a better person, weight loss, getting more exercise, weight loss, stop drinking alcoholic beverages, weight loss, and the list goes on.

When these got boring and tedious, as failure often is, I started coming up with a list of things I know I need help with and can actually measure success. *Be creative* I say to myself and so I usually start with something I think will be relatively simple. *I can do better* and *I will do better* have been my mantras and I actually believe in them. I really have. At the end of each year, I am at least able to tell myself I made a good try. Here's how each of the resolution methods have worked out:

I need at least three more hands to count how many years I've failed at the weight loss resolution. Yet every time I have made it my resolution, I've actually believed it was possible. Probably because I constantly changed the achievement factors. Instead of pounds, I'd shoot for inches. Or, instead of inches, I'd use ounces.

Losing 16 ounces sounded a lot better than one pound. Sometimes, instead of inches I used centimeters because they added up a lot faster. Even my goal sounded more fun: lose one meter. If I measured every part of my body, and I mean EVERY part of my body, one meter is achievable in about two months of dieting and working out. It's all about being creatively successful. At least that's how it works in my brain.

Yet, by about March I'd lose interest or motivation or energy or focus. This doesn't mean I don't keep trying to lose weight or get in shape. I just don't do it as a resolution anymore. It's too much pressure and I'm tired of failing miserably.

On other years I've begun with a deep breath and plenty of optimism. A personal favorite that has been tried many times is to get birthday cards and presents out to family and friends BEFORE their birthdays. Sounds simple. And doable. And yet, it never happens.

The problem with January birthdays is that I'm always still reeling with the trauma of Christmas and never think to buy any cards or presents with a birthday in mind. Even after many years of knowing the January birthdays were right after Christmas, I still manage to mess this one up on an annual basis. Not this particular year! I got both cards out on time and felt amazing.

I have a ton of birthdays to deal with in March. I use February to get prepared. In the 40+ years I've supposedly been an adult, I think I might have gotten all the cards and presents to the March birthday girls or boys on time twice. Twice I was amazing. I called the people I had sent the card and present to before their birthday to see if they had fainted when it arrived on time.

Sadly, the rest of the year's birthdays were all over the board, some early, some on time, most a wee bit late or a month late. I skipped some people altogether. So, I've tried different strategies like if someone's birthday was in June and they got my card and present within the month of June, it counted. Luckily, no one on my list had a birthday at the end of June. August is another big month in my world for family. Most of the time I did okay but I was an utter and complete failure with anyone who has a birthday from September to December.

At best, this is a resolution I continue to work on only not as a resolution. Just a challenge.

As far as resolutions went, I continued to be inept, from concept to when I would throw in the towel and declare myself unable to follow through. Again. I don't even know why I feel the need to make resolutions every year. It always seems like a good idea to do some targeted self-improvement. A new year feels like a new beginning where I get to start over fresh and make some a positive change.

I had to find a way to make success fun. I had a choice. A) I could either never make a resolution ever again for the rest of my life; B) I could make a resolution only on even or odd years; or C) I could come up with more interesting resolutions having nothing to do with the standard ones.

I was determined to use some focused criteria. Keep it simple, keep it meaningful, keep it small. In 2018 an idea hit me on New Year's Day. Ready?

I resolved not to buy any skin lotion for a whole year. There's a good reason this needed to be done.

I had scoured my house and truck for all my lotion bottles. When I had all of them corralled on the dining room table, I hung my head. How did I accumulate **fourteen** bottles of lotion without realizing I am a lotion hoarder? Uh oh, I hadn't counted all those little bottles or tubes I had taken from hotels. It was going to be more challenging than I thought possible. It was time to get a grip.

No matter how good it smelled or how it would reverse aging skin or hydrate, I was not going to continue to buy into the notion it was some kind of miracle lotion. I was going to give all my current bottles of lotion another chance to get it right, to do what they were supposed to do. No new lotion would cross the threshold of my life until all of what I had was gone, used up and the empty bottles thrown ceremoniously, including a little dance step, into the trash.

As with any resolution I have started by being seriously committed to, I came up with a battle plan. The bottles with the least amount of lotion would be used up first. I stationed them in four strategic places around the house and put one, and only one (not three), in my truck. The rest of the bottles I tucked away under the bathroom sink so I wouldn't be tempted to use them. I know how my mind works.

Right off the bat, I noticed a few problems with a couple of the almost empty ones. They were so old the color and smell had changed. The lotion also didn't want to come out of the bottles. I put them upside down. One of them sat for a week without budging. I threw it in the garbage. It's not cheating on the resolution if I couldn't get the stuff out.

I learned I had bought into the marketing strategy of brands using the words *'super dry skin'*, a common malady in the winter in Montana. One came out like that paste we used to have in elementary school back in the early 1960s. I smeared it on and waited for the miracle of supple skin. After about an hour, I realized it wasn't disappearing into the desert of my arm. I went and got a paint scraper and a roll of paper towels and commenced to remove it. That bottle ended up in the trash too.

The third bottle actually showed some promise. I put it on my other arm and rubbed it in. Pretty soon the rubbing in caused little Play-Doh wormlike pieces to form along the length of my forearm. What is this stuff, lotion or dried skin? I went outside and swept away all the little worms. That bottle also went bye-bye.

Three down, eleven to go. As with any good resolution, flexibility is the key to success. Modifying the rules along the way is part of learning more about myself and achieving something tangible. I would like to ask a favor though. If you happen to be anywhere near me and smell something kind of off, don't just back away. Tell me! Then I can get rid of another bottle. After I shower.

I stayed focused on this resolution throughout the year and managed to get rid of or use just about every bottle or tube in my possession. It wasn't until the end of 2020 that I actually got to buy a new bottle of lotion. It turned out to be a lot harder to decide what to get than I thought it would be. I actually thought about what I needed it to do and how it smelled. I spent a lot of time in the lotion aisles sniffing away, testing the consistency and reading what was in each one. I was so proud of myself and I plan to keep up the good work!

In 2019, I wracked my brain for another simple yet meaningful resolution. It came to me as I took a quart jug of milk out of the refrigerator and smelled it before pouring it in a glass. It was bad. I checked the expiration date and it was way beyond past due.

Milk will usually last a good week after the date so I was bad for not using it. As I thought about it, I realized how much milk I had thrown out in the last year and felt ashamed of myself. I love milk but apparently not enough to actually finish it before it gets icky. As I dumped the stuff down the sink and it came out in chunks, I had my new resolution. I will not throw any milk away for a year because I will drink it all before it curdles.

It went pretty well. I paid more attention to milk than any normal person should. I actually started to crave it a bit. Nothing quite as good as a glass of really cold milk. Yum! I thought of how it was helping me get some critical vitamins like D, always important in the winter in Montana. Or minerals like calcium where I hoped to improve my bone density results. Always on the lookout for positive results from my poor habits as a responsible consumer.

It was only problematic if I had to slug down more than half a jug right when I was leaving on a trip. Cold milk equals brain freeze. Despite that, I managed to finish off almost every milk jug in 2019 and now it is a habit. TAH DAH!

2020 was the year of eating breakfast. I have given short shrift to breakfast eating for years.

Breakfast is the most important meal of the day. It helps with blood sugar levels, improved metabolism, and all that junk. I know. I know. I know! It just hasn't been my morning priority like coffee, or letting the dogs out, or even thinking clearly. It takes me a while to wake up and even more time to make a decision about anything, much less what to eat.

I have been trying to make it easy. How hard is it to eat a breakfast bar? It's hard when I want bacon and eggs. But that requires cooking and dishes. I've had to fall back on old weight loss strategies like planning it out for the week and checking it off for accountability. I'm also working on variety like oatmeal, with or without fruit. Or yogurt, with or without fruit. Or scrambled eggs with spinach and no bacon. Okay, one strip of bacon.

Success has been sporadic. Good intentions are not a breakfast eaten. This resolution has been the toughest one yet which is exactly why it's needed. So, I will choke down food in the morning every day for the rest of the year. Stay tuned to see if this self-pep talk will do any good.

I think I'll find an easier resolution next year. Something simple like folding my clothes and putting them away as soon as the dryer is done drying them. Yeah, that sounds good. How hard can it be?

~ 21 ~

MUSIC GETS THE JOB DONE

Sometimes your helpers don't want you to sing so they let you know.

They are not very subtle.

Ever notice how your mind wanders when you are doing mindless tasks? What I notice most is how my brain fills the space with songs. Certain tasks beget certain genre.

For whatever reason, mowing the lawn brings out the disco queen in me. Donna Summers, KC and the Sunshine Band, the Bee Gee's, or Earth, Wind and Fire start fighting for attention. The jukebox of my memories shuffle. Sometimes Donna wins and one of her most epic songs is called *McArthur Park* and while I still don't know where it is, I feel like I need to go there. This is how it might go:

At the start of the song a few lines come into my head about how McArthur Park is melting and something about icing and then a ton of questions start popping up. Meanwhile, the music part is still playing. It's all supposed to be about mowing the dang yard. Who knew I was so coordinated?

As I mow, I'm wondering if it's sweet green icing or sweet cream icing? How does a park melt in the dark and why does it have icing? Where is it flowing down to? Why would you not be able to have a recipe again if you left the cake out in the rain? It's just a cake, why get so upset? Who even needs recipes? Get a grip people.

The song picks up speed in my head and the disco beat begins. I quickly realize I don't know any more lines in the song so I just keep repeating the cake lines, only faster. I'm singing away and fortunately for man, bird or beast, the mower is too loud to be heard above it. I hope. In nothing flat, the yard is done and I've performed a few mowing pirouettes I didn't even know it could do.

There have been times when I didn't get the lawn mowed in a timely fashion and it grew really tall. When this happened, I used the riding mower to get the first cut done. Then I used the push-and-grunt mower to clean it up to a more healthy, attractive look. I always have to make a decision about the artistry. Should I cross-hatch, chevron, or just go horizontal or vertical? What to do? What to do? So much pressure!

A decision is finally made and as I start, KC and the Sunshine Band starts singing *'Get Down Tonight'* in my head. Of course, all I remember is the chorus which has to do with dancing and making love. Makes me tired just thinking about it and since it's the same two lines over and over I'm pretty sure these are the only lyrics in this song. And someone made a lot of money, unlike writing a book. I need to let that go.

It doesn't take long before I am totally sick of those words. I try to come up with another song but the tune is so entrenched in my head, I can't think of one. I dump the grass from the now full grass catcher and pause to think, thus ending the mindless wandering for a brief moment. Finally, I decide to change the words to match the task at hand.

Cut a little grass, make it sort of short
It's looking good, it's looking good
Cut some more grass, keep the lines straight
It's looking good, it's looking good.

At some point in all this I am wondering if all the lyrics from that time period were inane. Really, all these songs are eight lines of lyrics that barely make sense and a ton of repetition with a catchy beat and musical notes. We loved them, danced to them, sang along. Huh. At least it didn't take up a lot of brain capacity to remember some of the words. It's always good to preserve memory space.

Before I know it, the lawn is beautiful. I pray I come up with a different song for next time. Disco is perfect for mowing the lawn. As I reflect on what I've accomplished, I realize I am grateful I didn't think of another KC and the Sunshine Band song like, '*Shake Your Booty.*'

People driving by my house might wreck.

Mowing the lawn isn't the only thing my head puts music to. I think I am the poster child for singing while I work. Or play. I have no idea why this happens. I don't even get to pick the songs; they pick me.

Every once in a while, I get the urge to repaint a room in my house. My painting song always seems to be Don McLean's *American Pie.* I'll be rolling paint on a wall, and it just pops into my head. The first time it happened, I realized it is one very long and complex song and I had no idea what order the stanzas came in and I was repeating myself a lot like a skipping record.

I've probably driven a Chevy to a levee about a million times now because the first line won't leave my brain. Every once in a while, another line comes out of nowhere and I start singing it over and over. For some reason I get stuck on moss growing fat and I'm visualizing how it could be possible if the stone is rolling. I am, after all, more of a scientist than a musician. Pretty sure that's not how it's supposed to be.

After repeating the line about forty times I realize I am making myself crazy. Parts of the wall I am painting have several coats of paint because I lost focus trying to figure out the song lyrics.

I put down the paint roller, walk out of the room and start looking for my *American Pie* record. Once I find it, I put it on the turntable and turn up the volume. (I love real records, scratches and all.) I return to my roller and sing along, from beginning to end. When the song ends, I go back and start it again. And again. Pretty soon, two walls are covered in new paint. Yes!

The song that has stirred my heart for decades became my painting soundtrack. The tempo is perfect for rolling in time. The walls are my masterpieces but McLean's song is a masterpiece for the ages. I can never listen to it without it bringing back memories of my high school days. The lyrics speak to the events of the 1960s and 1970s, when I was growing up.

I have no idea how or why it became my painting song. It doesn't really matter. All I know is that's the way I like it. Uh huh. Uh huh.

A note to the reader from the writer: If you are familiar with any of these songs, and they are now stuck in your head, you're welcome. If you haven't heard of any of these songs, you should check them out. We could sing them together!

22

SCORING THE DAY

Sometimes, scoring the day involves a selfie with a friend. This friend happened to be standing guard at a Buddhist temple in Laos. I knew I was safe even though it doesn't look like it. Trust issues?

Retirement has taken some time to get used to. One thing I've done to adapt to it is develop various strategies to focus on the goal of enjoying life now that I have a say in how each day will go. Some work and some don't. I love the illusion where I actually *think* I have a say. It gives me hope on a daily basis.

After my first cup of coffee, I usually wander around the house trying to decide what to get done before bedtime. I've discovered it's important to check my calendar so I don't forget to show up at some appointment or event. No one believes me when I tell them about how crazy busy retirement is. I literally have to schedule days, here and there, to just relax and read a good book or go camping, or for a hike somewhere with the dogs.

For the first several months of retirement I relied on getting things done by happenstance. I'd see the dishes in the sink and either wash them or put them in the dishwasher. I'd see the broom and sweep the floor. At some point I realized I was getting behind on the things I had to do to maintain the house because I kept choosing the things I wanted to do like work in the yard, go for a hike, play golf or hang out with friends. The outdoors always beats the indoors when it comes time to do anything. Hands down.

The funny thing about all this is that I used to do all these things while working a 40+ hour a week job. I barely kept up but I did it. Why is it so different now that I supposedly have more time? It is one of life's great mysteries, at least in my mind.

As I got further and further behind in the have to's, I started to feel helpless, overwhelmed, and bereft. It was much easier to see what I wasn't getting done than what I was getting done and after a while, I knew I needed a strategy.

My first strategy was sticky notes. I took my pad of sticky notes into each room and made a list of what needed to be done there. I slapped the note on some piece of furniture and moved to the next room until I had sticky notes everywhere. I still find them now and then and crumple them up. I don't even check to see what was on them. I just throw them away.

My second strategy, and the one I still use, was to get a great big whiteboard and attach it to the wall between the kitchen and the laundry room. I divided it into three columns to give the appearance that I possess some kind of organizational skills. I also purchased a set of multicolored dry erase pens and set them into a little bucket nearby. Using different colors would allow me to group like tasks or draw fun pictures while I was thinking of what to put on the list. I like to call the whole thing 'the GIANT white board'. Pretty good, huh?

Making the list was a lot harder than I thought it would be. I actually blanked out on what should go on it when I first started. I couldn't think of a thing to write. The board was so big. And so white. But once I got started, it was hard to stop writing. The list was GIANT.

I used to get overwhelmed and a little depressed by the extensiveness of the GIANT list until I started leaving the crossed-out stuff on there. I decided it was a good idea to leave more crossed out things on the list than to-do things because it made me feel super amazing. I even felt like someone should give me a gold star sometimes.

Retirement has its pro's and con's. Trying to figure out what day of the week it is can be both. Feeling like the days have meaning and purpose is so different from the days of having a regular job.

It's nice not to go to work but it doesn't mean I don't have a need for a sense of fulfilment. I realized I needed some kind of measuring stick for the days. Not a point accumulation thing. I don't want something requiring too much work or math. Yuck. No, not what I was looking for. I'm thinking of a qualitative score that focuses on the lessons and laughs of each day. And so, at the end of the day, I add it all up and consider that eternal question, *how was your day?*

Here are some examples of how it works:

I select something from the GIANT list that appears to be simple and straight forward: *deliver the trailer.* I had put my tent trailer up for sale on Craigslist and a family in Butte had come over to take a look at it a few days later. They wanted a day or so to decide. *(That's when I offered to deliver it if they did. I know how to sweeten a deal.)* A day or so later, they called back and said they wanted it so we picked a good day for both of us. Today was the day.

I backed the truck up to get it all hitched up and discovered I had performed a miracle. I had backed it up perfectly straight, hitch to ball. Things went downhill from there. The story of my life. It's not part of the plan when the ball on the hitch is higher than the receptacle on the trailer. It's supposed to be the other way around. The problem was, I hadn't noticed that the trailer had fallen off the block when the potential buyers had gone inside it. It was way too heavy to lift the trailer up by hand. I didn't have a jack that would lift it high enough. Uh oh.

Believing I was thinking clearly, I tried to roll the trailer back up onto a board nearby to make it higher and ended up rolling the trailer receptacle into the side of the ball with my hand in between. The pain was intense and I used a lot of bad words.

I sat down to think. Giving up is not what I do. Inspired by the hint of an idea, I started letting air out of the back tires of the truck until it went down enough to get the trailer onto the ball. Just like that, it was all hooked up. Then I got the air compressor and pumped the truck tires back up. Feeling a sense of accomplishment mixed with a tiny bit of pride, I pulled the trailer out of the garage, cleaned it out, made sure everything was hooked up properly and headed off to Butte. It was a beautiful day for a drive. I left the trailer at its new home and headed back.

The rest of the day and evening was productive but uneventful. That night, I stood at the GIANT whiteboard and crossed a few things off the list and added a few more. When I crossed out *deliver the trailer*, I used the fat part of the pen to make a fat line. SCORE! I looked at my hand and marveled that as painful as it was, I had been really lucky. It had been smashed at that little web area between the pointer and middle finger of my left hand. It could have smashed the bones and I could have been facing something broken. I am left-handed and it could have affected important things from typing to wiping. In reflection, it was a great day. I made mistakes. I did some things right. I learned a lot. I had moments of amazingness and humility. Mostly, humility. SCORE, SCORE, SCORE!

In the spring, I usually find myself wandering around the yard with a clipboard and pencil, making yet another list of all the things that need to be done. I transfer these to the now added 'outdoor' column on the GIANT whiteboard. Most of these are the things I tried to get done last year but got distracted by tasks that wouldn't be as painful or require as much thinking. I love it when I don't have to use my brain.

One day I selected *prune trees and shrubs.* It's a messy verb, pruning. It sounds simple and yet it requires careful consideration and technique. In practice I tend to draw blood, have branches fall on my head, and say 'whoops' a lot.

After I took a series of Master Gardening classes during the winter, I finally got brave enough to prune one of my apple trees. I studied the tree, circling it like some kind of famous sculptor, cutting off limbs and branches until I had shaped it nicely. I was pretty pleased with myself and felt like I was doing it a huge favor. After all, I had paid attention, taken notes in class and even gotten a good score on the test.

The apple tree died. Seriously, it did.

I later discovered it had nothing to do with my pruning technique. It died from the effects of a late hard frost the fall before and it was doomed before I even touched it. Whew. Timing can be everything.

Scoring the day may not be immediately obvious. Sometimes, it comes in a few weeks or months when I notice the results of pruning other trees or shrubs I did correctly. Speaking of pruning, that reminds me, I need a haircut. Good thing I have the GIANT white board.

It doesn't always have to be about big things or anything relating to the GIANT whiteboard. When I take stock of the day, it's the little things that add up. I'll tally up little reminders of what went right in the day versus what went wrong. Both can add to the score in ways I am never expecting.

For example, one day I had a ton of shopping to do while my little dog was at the groomer. I was zipping around town picking up this and that and as I left Wal-Mart, I realized I had somehow gotten a cart where all the wheels worked perfectly throughout the whole shopping experience. That had never happened before. I didn't even know it was possible. SCORE!!

Yup, scoring the day can happen anytime and in ways I never expect. I can go into all kinds of interesting detail about how I rented a Caterpillar skid steer tractor with a bucket for a day on my birthday one year. I scored all kinds of things; the ground, a fence (whoops), a whole row of shrubs. The true score was the gigantic smile on my face the whole time. My teeth dried out from all that smiling.

The secret to happiness is in paying more attention to the good things that happen in any given day. Every single day has them even when it feels like nothing has gone right. My scoring 'system' works for me. It makes me laugh at myself more than cry, my heart feels happy, and I share the joy every chance I get. Some people find me annoying that way. SCORE!!

23

WHO OWNS WHO?

Corgi and kitty love. Cuteness overload.

I have been blessed, throughout my life, with a plethora of pets. Growing up, we had everything from turtles to parakeets, chickens to pheasants, cats and dogs, a mouse and a hamster. We even had an ant farm though I wouldn't call ants pets. There are too many to give names to and what's a pet without a name?

In my adult life, I've kept the assortment to just dogs and cats. Unlike many of the other kinds of pets, they have a longer shelf life. And individual personalities. I fall deeply and ridiculously in love with each one. In my world they are not animals, they are family.

As I write this, Tank my 2-year-old Corgi Australian shepherd mix, is staring at me from across the room on his little couch. It's as if he knows I'm writing about him. I'm pretty sure he wants to make sure I get it right. He's handsome and amazing and that's all anyone needs to know. His words, not mine. I have recently put a blanket down on the little couch to protect it and to make him comfy. When he's done staring at me and checking for anything out of place, he spins around a few times, arranges the blanket with his teeth and front paws, and then settles down and goes to sleep. With one eye open. Just in case I leave the room without him or I feel the need to pay attention to anyone but him. He's a wee bit needy.

Joseph Kitty, one of my two cats, lies next to me whenever I'm on the computer. We have a routine in place where he sees me head to my writing place most mornings with a cup of coffee. After I sit down, he crouches down in front of the chair like he's trying to decide which side he will jump up from. If he jumps up from my right, he is telling me to move the coffee cup or risk disaster. Even though the space I've made for him is on my left, he almost always insists on jumping up from the right. I'm pretty sure it's so he can slowly walk across my computer to get to his happy place. He then nestles along my left leg, starts purring, yawns, and goes to sleep.

After a couple coffee spills and some interesting words or paragraphs he created while standing on various computer keyboard keys, I've learned to accept this routine and have made the appropriate adjustments. He knows he is my writing muse and I think he's trying to tell me he should be acknowledged as my co-author. Got it.

Both Joseph Kitty and Tank, my boys, assist and protect me while I write. It's a serious and dangerous job but they seem up to the task. Oh, they may look like they're sleeping but a keen observer would note their eyes are never totally closed.

Meanwhile, I have no idea where the girls are. They'll show up sometime during the day and expect something from me, maybe a good rubdown or food. Maizy, my 3-year old Corgi, is a tiny girl and I find myself talking nonsense to her about how she's my little wiggle. I speak in a voice I would not recognize as my own if I were to hear it recorded and played back to me. In this, I know I'm not alone. I have yet to meet a pet owner that doesn't alter the tone of his/her voice when talking to a furry kid. It's endearing, sometimes bordering on nauseating.

Little Zoe, sister to Joseph Kitty, is my outdoor helper. No matter what the task, she wants to help. If I'm loading my little truck to take things to the dump, she sits on top of the cab. If I sit down to weed one of the raised beds in the garden, she lies next to me and stretches so I'll rub her tummy. If I stop, she settles down under the asparagus plants and takes a nap. Not fair, I want a nap too.

Our life is full of ritual and routine. We've built it over time, and I've come to realize how much I rely on the presence of each one of them. I marvel at every nuance and individual quirkiness that make up our relationships to one another.

When I first got the kitties, they started off with the names, Joey and Zoey. They were tiny fluffs of energy and claws. To get their attention, I used what I call my ultrasonic voice. I emit a sound that is at the highest register of my voice. I don't have to use words but I do so it's not unusual to see or hear a response to *'little baby kitties'* in the key of really squeaky (think of the sound of the air being let out of a balloon really slowly). If either are nearby, I get a different response depending on who it is. Little Zoe, aka Zoey, will come trotting to me, tail straight up, with a look of great expectation. I'm not sure what she expects but she looks so excited. I choose to interpret it as she is happy to see me. Joseph Kitty, aka Joey, talks back. In fact, he talks back from wherever he is to wherever I am. He seems to come to me in slow motion so I call him Mr. Lug. At some point in his approach, I lose patience and turn my back. It doesn't seem to bother him at all. He'll get to me when he's ready and not a moment sooner.

Maizy has the kitties trained better than I do. She uses them to clean her face. The first time I saw her do this, I thought it was the cutest thing I'd ever seen. There was Little Zoe lying in the middle of the rug. Maizy walked up and plopped herself down right in front of Zoe's head. She put her head on Zoe's front legs and waited. Nothing happened so she scooted closer. Pretty soon Zoe got busy cleaning Maizy's eyes, nose, ears and the top of her head. She stopped so Maizy cleaned one of Zoe's ears and then put her head back in play for more cleaning. It doesn't matter what I'm doing, I can't help but watch until one of them gets up and walks away. Recently, I noticed she has Joseph Kitty attending to her face too. I'm not going to lie, it's always adorable.

One of our nightly routines involves catnip. I walk over to a cabinet thingy in my living room and pull out a drawer. Instantly the kitties come running from wherever they are in the house. This excites Tank so he has to come over too. I pull out the bag of catnip and dispense a little pile for each kitty making sure they aren't too close to each other. Joseph Kitty eats a bit of his, sneezes, and then rolls in it. Little Zoe sits and eats hers until it's all gone, like the little princess she is. Meanwhile, Tank is inching his way toward them because he loves catnip too. I've explained countless times to him that it is CATnip, not DOGnip. He does not care. He will clean up any and every bit of whatever is left over. Fortunately, it doesn't seem to affect him the way it does the cats. Their dilated pupils are creepy.

After catnip time, I turn off all the lights except the ones in my bedroom. Then I go into the bathroom to brush my teeth. Every one of them is there to make sure I'm doing it right. At least that's what I think they are thinking. When I make the before-bed potty stop, all four of them have followed along. I'm pretty sure this is the only place I could actually take a selfie of all of us together. The second I reach for the toilet paper they all take off like their rear ends are on fire. Note to self: the next house I live in will have a door between the bedroom and the bathroom.

We have a bedtime routine too and it starts the second I am ready to climb into bed.

Everyone gets up on the bed. They all try to get on my legs and lap. In no time I'm pinned to the bed unable to move. As soon as I pick up a book, two of the four relocate somewhere else on the bed. Whew. Maizy has her own pillow next to mine and she snuggles in with at least one part of her touching me. Tank moves to the end of the bed and gnaws on one his many bones. Joseph Kitty lies on my legs, stretched out in contentment. Little Zoe lies on my lap and purrs. All is well in our little world.

When I turn off the light to go to sleep, I realize just how heavy two kitties can be. Neither wants to give up their comfy place and as I attempt to settle down in my own comfy place, it feels like I have to move two 50-pound sacks off me just to slide down into a prone position. Neither tries to help at all. I am forced to roll them off me and once I finally get settled, they rearrange themselves on top of me again. Should I try to roll over, I feel their stares in the dark reminding me to hurry up and quit moving. Not for the first time I wonder how they'd like it if I laid on top of them. I'm getting good at rolling my eyes in the dark.

By morning, the kitties are gone and as soon as I move, both dogs pounce on me in glee. I quickly flip onto my stomach and let them dance on my back. I put the pillow over my head and they take turns trying to dig me out and clean my face. I may not be a morning person but they have a way of making me wake up a little more willing to leave the comfort of a nice warm bed. Who could not be touched by their joy and happiness?

One of the main reasons I love to hike is because of the dogs. Their short little legs don't stop them from going anywhere they want to go. Tank is all over the place, running and boinging through the tall grass. It's almost as if his legs are on pogo sticks. He can hear a mouse sneeze a hundred yards away and will leap into the air with the expectation of catching it. Sometimes he actually does and he looks at me with surprise and a *'What do I do now?'* expression.

Meanwhile, Maizy walks about 20 yards in front of me on whatever trail we're following. If she gets caught up in one of Tank's crazy moments and gets further ahead of me, she stops to make sure she can see me before she follows him. I don't know if she's my protector or if she just doesn't want to get lost. I'll probably never know for sure but I'm going to go with her being my protector. It makes me feel more loved.

The three of us have covered a lot of ground over the years. It doesn't matter where we go, the joy of untethered freedom is hard to beat. I love to just stop walking and watch them zip around, smelling everything along the way. The only time the silence is broken is when one of them finds something really disgusting to roll in and then my voice can be heard echoing for miles. Usually, it's something dead but it can also be some particularly fresh and fragrant animal excrement (poop). I'll never understand why dogs, who have such acute smell abilities, find disgusting smells something they have to add to their bodies.

Maizy is way smarter than Tank. How do I know? To date, he has attacked and lost to one skunk and two porcupines. She has shown no inclination to do anything so dumb. In fact I'm pretty sure I've seen her shake her head and mutter *'moron.'*

Once, while walking through the snow near the Missouri River, Tank stopped in his tracks and started barking like a crazed maniac. I thought for sure it was something like a bear or a moose, maybe even a mountain lion. Maizy and I looked towards what we thought he was barking at. It turned out to be an old cottonwood tree that had fallen over, the remaining trunk sticking up about three feet in the air. As we walked toward it, he got more agitated. Finally, Maizy jumped up on the length of the fallen tree and walked to the stump and just stood there. She seemed to be telling him, *'Look at me. I'm taller than you and a lot smarter.'* If a dog could look ashamed, he did. I later wondered if I should get him eyeglasses.

I cannot imagine my life without pets. I don't want to. Every moment I get to spend with them is full of love and brings joy and entertainment to my life. I once asked my vet if she would consider putting me to sleep one day when I get too old to have a pet or two. She looked at me, shook her head and said, *'No Shelley, I can't do that.'* She might have thought I was joking. I was not. For all my furry family gives me, life would not be as rich and entertaining without them. We all know the hardest part of having them is losing them. No matter how much it hurts they are more than worth it.

It's no secret they bring out the best in me. It doesn't matter how many of them come and go in my lifetime, I am humbled and grateful for every one of them and every moment we share.

Dedicated to Peanuts, Tenaya, Cooper, Ted, Rowdy, Splatty, Hannah, Sassy, Brody, Joseph, Zoe, Maizy, Phoebe and Tank.

24

GOLF- A FOUR-LETTER WORD FOR A REASON

In case it isn't obvious, this is me when I realized I had gotten a
HOLE IN ONE!
Thus proving golf is all about miracles. And dorks.

I don't know if any other golfer has picked up on this but the game of golf is full of four-letter words. Flag, ball, putt, shot, cart, fore, club, iron, wood, fade, chip, hole, hook, play, etc. Words I might use while playing the game tend to be ones my Little Mother would wash my mouth out with soap if she heard me. They just slip out even when I've tried to replace them with DANG, SPIT, or HECK.

I've been playing golf for a long, long time with decades of interruptions.

My introduction to golf came about when Dad did his tour in Vietnam and the rest of us briefly moved to a beach community in southern California. The backyard looked out on a golf course and that is where my brother Bruce (age 10) and I (age 11) got our first taste of golf. Our house was situated at the junction of four holes with a lake in play on all of them. Every late afternoon found us down by the lake looking for golf balls. We also found golf clubs in the lake. It was the first hint about how maddening the game could be.

When Dad got back from Vietnam, we moved to Clark Air Force Base in the Philippines. There was a great golf course there with an $8 per month family rate. Dad, Bruce, and I tried to learn how to play, using rental clubs, and guessing how it was supposed to work. We were rescued from our efforts by the caddies we were required to use. They were local Filipino people who carried our clubs from hole to hole and schooled us on how to hit, what clubs to use and the rules of the game. They definitely knew their stuff and thankfully shared it, probably because they felt sorry for us. As we got better, the game became almost enjoyable.

After two years in the Philippines, we were reassigned to McChord AFB in Tacoma, Washington. In the summers, Dad would drop us off at the base golf course on his way to work and pick us up on his way home. For about 2 years, Bruce and I carried our bags, walked miles and miles, and smacked that little white ball all over the place. Playing 36 holes of golf a day, we got pretty good. If we kept score, Bruce beat me regularly but I didn't care after a while. Plus, I'm pretty sure he cheated....

At this point in our lives, we had reached the early teen years. I don't remember us ever using four-letter words when we golfed. Maybe it was because we spent a lot of time golfing with Dad and we didn't dare use them. Maybe we didn't know how or what words to use. I don't know. In retrospect, I don't know how we didn't use them but they weren't part of the game I remember. I wonder what we said.

Dad retired from the Air Force in my sophomore year of high school. We moved to a small town in northern California. Golf pretty much disappeared from my life. There was no golf course nearby so I took up dating, and sports like basketball and softball. Seems logical, right? Then, I went to college, got a job, and moved around some more. For decades, I didn't golf. My little orange golf bag and real wood golf clubs followed wherever I moved and never got used.

I finally moved to a small town in Montana with a golf course when I was in my mid 30s but I didn't seriously pick it up again until I was in my 50s. To say I was a bit rusty is an understatement. My clubs were sorely outdated and my old bag was cracked. I upgraded them because, as any golfer worth their salt will tell you, it's about the equipment, not the person. Lessons? Who needs lessons? I'll just practice and play. A lot. It's like riding a bike. Right? Um, not exactly.

I like to describe our little course as the flattest, straightest golf course in the world with no water hazards and tiny greens shaped like turtle shells. You would think its lack of complexity would make it easier for me to get back in my golf groove. My golfing muscle memory was long gone and it was like starting over. It took a while, but I improved enough to want to keep playing. To this day I have rounds where I question that decision.

Here's the thing about golf that is inescapable. We all start a round of golf with a ton of optimism. At the first tee, we stretch and contemplate where we want to hit the ball for maximum advantage in addressing the second shot. That's what you do in golf, address the ball. Who comes up with this lingo? Anyway, the tee goes into the ground, the ball is placed precariously on top of it, several practice swings later, the time comes to actually hit the ball. Optimism is still part of the thinking. Reality can go one of two ways. I know because I've lived it. To simplify, the first hit of the round will either be really good or super bad.

If the first shot is really good, it seems to follow that the next shot will be really bad. I don't know why. For the rest of the round, it's a crap shoot. It doesn't matter how it feels when I'm standing there, ready to hit the ball, I feel like I've done all the necessary mechanical, mental and emotional self-talk and it's going to be a perfect shot. As I slowly take the club back, I feel one with the ball. My eyeballs are lasered in. At just about the moment of contact, a tiny bit of doubt creeps in and any one of a million wrong things make it so the ball goes nowhere near where I thought I was aiming.

One of the smartest things I ever did in golf was join other people who play like I do. We share a common misery or celebrate shots we never knew we had in us. All of us try really hard to play well as opposed to needing some timely luck to keep us from quitting.

We cheer each other on and find creative ways to say something positive about a terrible shot. Every one of us has at least one 'hell' hole during a round. For some reason, the golf karma dude in each of our heads decides to take a nap and selects a random hole where every single shot on a particular hole is horrible. It gets really quiet. There is nothing to say or do but gut it out to the pin. Pity is another four-letter word felt during a hell hole.

Having spent a lot of time either playing golf or because I live near a golf course there are two four-lettered-words I hear pretty regularly. One starts with an 'S' and the other is 'F'. Angst, frustration, and rage all form the expletive issued forth. Sometimes very loudly and since sound carries pretty far, everyone on the course or the back decks of any of the houses along the course, knows when things are not going well for someone.

So, what is it about golf that makes it so emotional? I could write a book about it but instead I'm going to try to simplify it.

It's hard.

There are so many facets about the game that are way different than any other sport. The only real commonality is they are pretty much all played with a ball. That's it. The golf ball is tiny in comparison to those other sports. And every golf course is set up differently. Trees, sand, short grass, long grass, and water are spread over 9 or 18 holes in combinations where a ball that is 1.68 inches in diameter needs to end up in a 4.25-inch diameter hole. To do that, there are all kinds of clubs designed to do different things to hit the ball into the hole from a measured distance away in as few hits as possible.

Along the way, from the tee box to the hole, there are obstacles like the aforementioned water, sand, and trees. In my experience, the trees have embedded magnets connected to the balls. I've never seen the equations involved in the direction any ball will take after hitting a tree but I bet even the most brilliant minds in statistics and physics would shudder. A water feature, whether lake, stream or ditch send waves of sounds to the balls enticing them to join together. The sand traps are designed to remind you that if you thought golf couldn't get worse, it really can. The good news is any sand leaving the trap with the ball will go in your eyes so you will have a good excuse to play poorly for the rest of the round.

It's frustrating.

I don't remember ever feeling frustrated or angry playing golf in my younger years. Starting to play decades later brought out a whole new me, not necessarily a pleasant me. It sometimes feels next to impossible to have two amazing shots in a row. More often than not, it takes several holes to have a great shot. Just when I'm ready to throw my clubs in a water feature or at someone, miracles happen and a shot might be more than great. I actually got a hole-in-one once. I did. Every once in a while, I've been known to chip the ball into the hole from various distances from off the green. I always stand in amazement and awe, with my mouth hanging open like I can't believe it happened. It's not one of my more attractive looks. I can hear my dad saying '*Close your mouth, you look like a fish.*'

It's cathartic.

The real gift of golf is its ability to allow one to express real emotion quickly and let it go. No leftover baggage. Emotions run the gamut of overwhelming joy to the depths of despair. Whatever it is, it is erased by the result of the next shot.

Pretty much every time I play golf, I ask myself why. Is it the colorful language I use? Is it actually fun? Am I getting a lot of exercise? Am I spending quality time with friends? Am I getting any better? Does it matter?

I think I just crave that feeling of a good solid shot. Whether it's a great drive, a 60-foot putt, or a perfect fairway wood hit, there's such a miracle about a little white ball going hundreds of yards from point A to point B, into a 4.25-inch hole. It's crazy.

As I bend down to tee the ball up, I realize this is a sport that keeps on giving. Invisible bubbles of four-letter words spring out of my head. *Hope!* This time the ball is going to go far and straight. *Fore!* Whoops, it didn't go straight. *Ball!* I blame you for not listening. *Love!* I actually love this game despite how it sounds. *Golf!* The ultimate mind-game. *Amen!*

By the way, golf spelled backwards is **FLOG**. How fitting.

We have flogging down really well. It's important to be good at something in this game.

25

COMING HOME

My home until I come home.

Apparently, I'm not going anywhere.

I'm a chronic adventurer, and as much as I love seeing new places, I also love coming home. As soon as I begin the trek back to real life, my mind and heart look forward to this final part of the trip. It doesn't matter if I'm gone for a couple days or a couple weeks, that first glimpse of my town and then my house, sets off fireworks of emotions, all happy. Goosebumps may be involved. Sometimes even tears.

In my world, there are two kinds of adventures. Both have their pros and cons and I wrestle with guilt or responsibility either way.

One is where I have to fly somewhere. This means I have to leave my furry kids at home. They all know when the suitcase comes out, I will disappear for some length of time without them. I still haven't figured out if it's better to start packing right before I leave or days before I leave. The suitcase brings instant sadness to the kitties and doggies and guilt to me.

I've tried it both ways but somehow, they know. Joseph Kitty can be found lying in my suitcase, front paws curled up into his chest and eyes closed, like a Zen kitty. Little Zoe will get into an open suitcase and try to make a nest by throwing clothes out and turning circles before settling down and then looking at me with an expression of *'You aren't going anywhere.'*

The doggies, on the other hand, are like night and day. Tank becomes Mr. Velcro. I can't go anywhere without him dogging (ha ha) my every move. Maizy turns into little Miss Distant. She can either be found under the bed, on the floor of my closet, or sitting and staring woefully at me from afar.

As I load the truck to go to the airport, my heartstrings are pulled in every direction. It sucks. I throw every kind of treat in the house at them like candy at a parade to assuage my guilt. The kitties get enough catnip to make them catatonic and the doggies get dog biscuits and rawhide chewies. I tell myself they are fine. I always want to go back and check to see if they are.

At the end of the trip, when I drive home from the airport, my heart is singing because I know I will see them all soon. I pull up to the house, open the garage door and prepare myself for the best kind of welcome home ever. I can hear the doggies as I get out of the truck. I open the door and they look at me, there's a brief pause and then, wham-o, glee! *'Yay!! You're home! We missed you!!!'*

I wander through the house like I've been gone for a year instead of a week or so, moving from room to room, taking it all in. The kitties make their appearances in their own sweet time, like felines do. My heart is getting fuller by the second. As I head for the back door to the yard, I make a pitstop, giving them all time to catch up to me. As soon as I reach for the toilet paper, they race to the door. It's like a Pavlovian response but instead of a bell, it's toilet paper roll noise.

I open the door and they race outside like their little rear ends are on fire. I stand on the deck and take in the view, breathing deeply and making happy whimpering noises. I can't help it. I am home and I never feel more grateful for it than in that moment.

The other kind of adventure, and I have to say I'm especially partial to it, is the camping trip one. I spend weeks getting ready for it. I've dreamed about the destination for months. I load my little Rpod teardrop trailer with clothing for any kind of weather. I have maps and books about the area I plan to investigate. I have more food than I could possibly eat but I can't help it. I've cleaned every nook and cranny in the little trailer, checked tires and batteries, made sure everything works that's supposed to, and gone through my checklist about a hundred times.

Instead of being sad, the doggies are beyond excited. They know they always get to go camping and it is, by far, their favorite thing in the whole wide world. I've taught them well. They race into the trailer, out of the trailer, up on the bed, down off the bed, countless times. Even the kitties come inside. They like to explore from top to bottom. They don't get to go but they still like the trailer. To be fair, I did take them once and we both decided camping is not their thing.

After a week or two of seeing and staying in some of the most beautiful places in the western part of our country, we begin our journey home. I pull the plug on the clean water tank and watch as we dribble down the highway. There is an internal threshold I reach when it's time to go home and I always listen to it. Home is calling and I must go. The doggies are exhausted and pass out in the back seat. I always wish I could pass out in the back seat but that is never in the cards. Instead, I start thinking about all the things I will need to do when I get home. Already, I'm transitioning from fun to real life.

As soon as we hit the dirt road to the house, both doggies jump up and get excited. They know where we are and can't wait to check out the house and yard to see what's been going on while they were away.

I back the trailer up as close to the garage as I can without hitting it, put the doggies in the house, and then head back to unhook, gather up garbage, dirty clothes, and uneaten food. Instead, I stop and walk over to the middle of the front yard. I slowly turn all the way around, taking in everything around me. Movement catches my eye and both kitties come trotting up, tails pointed to the sky, little sounds of happiness coming from each of them. I sit down in the grass and give them my undivided attention for a few minutes. Then, the trip memories begin to fade as I start to assess real life again. Mow the lawn, start some laundry, check the fridge for what's there to fix for dinner, and go through the mail. It can all wait as I fall back onto the grass and revel in the love of happy kitties.

No matter where I've been, how I got there, what I saw and got to do, one of the best parts of any trip is coming home.

It may be why I go.

~ 26 ~

CHANGING THE WORLD

MINIONS!!!

I've been thinking and I've come up with a way to change the world for the better. It's very simple. Superhero or animated cartoon underwear for boomers. Yup. It's past the time to bring back the characters from the 50s and 60s. Who is with me?

Not one to let a great idea go, I thought about the travesty of there not being any relevant fun underwear for boomers, especially women. I might have seen men's boxers at a box store with Batman or whoever the latest Marvel superhero is on them, but nothing I could relate to. And I don't wear boxers. Maybe I should.

In no time, memories of my childhood cartoon heroes popped up over my head in little balloons faces: Popeye, Rocky and Bullwinkle, Dudley Do-Right, Underdog and my favorite, Mighty Mouse! Superheroes galore! All had one mission. Making the world a better place, saving it from evil, taking care of all the bad guys, and untying helpless women from train tracks.

Starting my day with a fresh pair of matched socks, underwear and sports bra featuring Mighty Mouse after wearing some Underdog pajamas during the night would put a smile on my face nothing could take away. There would be nothing I couldn't do. Or at least try to do. Aging boomers need to feel like anything is possible, even though it will probably hurt.

For several nights, when I tried to fall asleep this superhero underwear idea kept pinging around in my head, and I began to come up with marketing ideas. For example, with your 3-pack of Popeye themed stuff, you would get a sticker to put on your car or hard side luggage. The sticker would be a can of opened spinach. Hmm, since most people don't like canned spinach like I do, it would have to have Popeye's hand squishing it and the top popping up just like he does before he eats it and becomes super strong. And since it is on my luggage, I'd find it in no time on any airport carousel and mightily lift it so it doesn't go around again. Yeah, that's an image I could get behind. Unfortunately, I'd probably have the Popeye song stuck in my head for hours.

Or, each package comes with a miniature toy of the character that everyone would want to collect and save. It could be displayed in a tasteful case that hangs on the wall so your friends could admire your collection and wonder what you are wearing that day. If that's not a conversation starter, I don't know what is. Because we are boomers and learned nothing from our parents, we would save all of these things for our kids to throw away later. And because we are mindful of the environment, these toys would be biodegradable AND provide critical nutrients to the soil.

Of course, all these cartoons had more than the featured heroes who saved the day. Who can forget Popeye's friend, Wimpy? I see hamburger themed everything. Or the girlfriends, never wives, of Popeye's Olive Oyl, or Dudley Do Right's Nell? Mighty Mouse's Pearl Pureheart? Now I'm wondering why no one was ever married in these cartoons.

The biggest problem in coming up with these brilliant ideas is focusing in on how to make it happen. I'm easily distracted by side thoughts. The people who came up with these cartoons in the first place were incredibly creative. For example, the Rocky and Bull-winkle show had a whole bunch of fun characters like the evil Boris and Natasha who called their nemesis characters 'Moose and Squir-rel' in Russian accents. If I wore Boris and Natasha socks one day, would it give me license to be evil that day? Would I start talking in a Russian accent? That could be a clear warning to people to leave me alone. Of course, I'd have to take my shoes off to make it clear about my mood. Maybe talking with an accent would be enough. Using an accent is about as bilingual as I get.

Other characters in the show like Sherman and Peabody, the brainiac dog and his boy, tried to change the world with their brilliance. By wearing the socks, and regular clothes of course, I could solve all kinds of problems for other people. If I wear the socks, underwear and bra, it would be a day I'd feel super amazing and helpful. If we had a Sherman and Peabody Underwear Day, think of all the great things we could accomplish.

Should it take a while to get the boomer heroes clothing on the market, whenever a new animated movie comes out, there should be a law that states that if there are kids clothing produced as a result of said movie, corresponding adult clothing should also be available. Okay, maybe not a law but a good business practice would be highly encouraged.

I came to this conclusion while I was shopping for clothing for my 7-year-old niece. As I wandered down the aisles of Walmart in the girl's socks and underwear section, I noticed that there were themes for everything from Dora the Explorer to Paw Patrol to Hello Kitty, Bob the Builder, and Lego Batman. It further supported my idea about what was lacking in the adult world.

Since I love going to the animated movies at the theatre, I like to take my 90-year-old Little Mother so I'm not alone. She goes for the popcorn and I go for the inspiration. For the longest time I became a Despicable Me groupie. I can wear little kids socks because I have little feet and have been known to purchase themed socks just to feel one with my minions. Who doesn't smile when they see Minions on their feet?

Oh, and another good business practice, why is it that kids are the only ones getting cool bedding, including sleeping bags? I could easily see myself camping with an adult sized Yogi and Boo Boo sleeping bag. Perhaps, it would keep the less friendly bears away. That's a stretch but maybe not. It's never been tried. And I am not volunteering.

I'm pretty sure I would wake up every day feeling like I could conquer the toughest job successfully if I had Moana bedding. She actually did save the world with the help of a chicken, Hei Hei, and a spirit guy, Maui, who had lost his mojo until she showed up. She's my hero in today's movies for kids.

I could go on and on about all of this but alas, I must go do adult stuff like vacuuming. Maybe I'll wear my minion socks to make sure I do a good job.

Shelley lives in Townsend, Montana with her furry friends, Corgis Maizy and Tank along with kitties, Zoe and Phoebe. She's been retired since 2011 and has had no problem finding ways to stay busy. This is her second book, the first being *Did I Say That Out Loud?* which received nothing but 5-star ratings on Amazon. She also has a website, shelleydouthett.com where she blogs and reveals more about life in retirement in a thoughtful and humorous way.

The author and her kids
photo by Dawn Alsop

9 798218 195984